300

Running poorly costs more than you realize...

TUNE UP YOUR MARRIAGE

Gary L. Vaughn, PhD

Anderson, Indiana

Coordinator of Publishing & Creative Services
Church of God Ministries, Inc.
PO Box 2420
Anderson, IN 46018-2420
800-848-2464
www.chog.org

To purchase additional copies of this book, to inquire about distribution, and for all other sales-related matters, please contact:

 Warner Press, Inc.
PO Box 2499
Anderson, IN 46018-2499
800-741-7721
www.warnerpress.org

Cover and text design by Mary Jaracz
Edited by Joseph D. Allison and Stephen R. Lewis

ISBN-13: 978-1-59317-370-8

Library of Congress Cataloging-in-Publication Data

Vaughn, Gary L.
  Tune up your marriage / Gary L. Vaughn.
    p. cm.
  ISBN 978-1-59317-370-8 (hardcover)
  1. Marriage--Religious aspects--Christianity. I. Title.
BV835.V39 2009
248.8'425--dc22   2009008849

Printed in Canada.

06 07 08 09 10 / TC / 10 9 8 7 6 5 4 3 2 1

CONTENTS

ACKNOWLEDGMENTS

I have discussed writing a book with my wife for many years. There were so many marriage books already out there, did we really need one more? But as I counseled couples over the years, I felt the need to reach out to married men. It is often the man who procrastinates when it comes to getting help in a marriage. Many couples have asked if I had written anything that would help them remember what we had discussed in counseling sessions or marriage seminars. It started with some handouts, grew into a couple of pamphlets, and finally developed into this book. I felt led to help couples, especially men, get their marriages in gear and live joyously with their spouses.

I give my first thanks to the Lord for the strength and encouragement he has given me throughout my career and this process. I found encouragement and practical knowledge in Terrie Squires. I knew next to nothing about the publishing world. She is credited with getting everything rolling. Mary Collette was a treasure in helping me organize my written thoughts into something more literary. Tammy White listened to endless dictations while typing my first manuscript. I thank her for her patience. Shalimar Scott has been an encouraging friend and coworker. To my partners and colleagues at Anderson Family Practice, thank you for your prayers and encouragement. I thank Dr. Donald Joy, who spent time correcting my first chapters. He also willingly shared his wisdom and insight about writing with a rookie. My many thanks to Joe Allison, acquisition editor for adult books at Warner Press, who took me by the hand and led me through this process. His patience and kindness have been such a blessing. To Stephen Lewis, your writing skills and corrections are what made this book what it is today, thank you. Finally, I wish to thank my family, who have prayed for this book from start to finish. Thanks guys! God has blessed me with the best kids ever. To my wife, Debby, words can never express what you mean to me; you are truly a godly woman in every way. You made this book come alive and real in all the insights you provided. I love you.

1. WARNING LIGHTS ARE FLASHING

1. WARNING LIGHTS ARE FLASHING
RESTORING LOVING COMMITMENT AND SACRIFICE

"In this same way, husbands ought to love their wives as their own bodies. He who loves his wife loves himself." —Ephesians 5:28

Bill and Ellie had been married for fifteen years. They met in college on a mission trip and were married soon after graduation. Bill took a job with a publishing company while Ellie started teaching fourth grade. After two years, Ellie quit teaching to stay home with their first child, Sarah. Little Joey and Will were born within the next few years. Bill was successful but had to travel quite a lot. Ellie loved being a mother, but she began to feel lonely. She thought she just needed adult conversation. Once the children entered school, Ellie went back to teaching. She enjoyed teaching, but there was still a void in her life.

At lunch one day, the fifth-grade teacher commented that she seemed down. She gradually began to share her feelings with him. He was so interest*ed*, and interest*ing*. She felt a little guilty, so she told Bill all she had shared with Ted, without mentioning Ted. Ellie thought that if she and Bill could reconnect everything would be better. But Bill just nodded and then told her the troubles he was having with his two current projects.

Ellie loved her children and wanted a secure home for them. She and Bill never fought, but she was just so sad—no, worse than sad, she felt empty of any feeling, at least for Bill. She wanted to laugh and play again. Was this all her marriage was ever going to be? She had prayed for something to change, but she felt so distant from her husband. She finally told Bill that she thought it would be better for everyone if they divorced.

Bill was stunned. He had been unaware of any problem in their marriage. This conversation brought them to my office.

Ellie sat very erect, hands folded, at the edge of the couch. She looked straight in front of her, avoiding the two pairs of eyes searching her face. What was she seeing, I wondered: her marriage to Bill, someone else, or the nothingness that her features expressed?

I asked Ellie why she wanted out of their marriage. Her answer came in a flat monotone: "I just don't love him anymore. It seems that all my feelings for him have disappeared. They've slowly evaporated into the air, and they're gone. My decision wasn't a sudden impulse. I was sad about our relationship for a long time, but now I just don't care."

Bill straightened from his corner of the couch. His whole body registered the shock and dismay of the last few days. He couldn't believe this was happening. They were good Christians. He didn't know what was wrong with her. Sure, they had some problems, but so did most couples. How had it come to this? He tried to get her to look at him. Taking her hand, he searched her face, but she averted her eyes.

"Gone? How can it just be gone?" he asked. "Fifteen years and your love just 'evaporated' into thin air? I'm sorry, Ellie, I just don't understand. Help me to understand. Won't you give me another chance? Won't you even try?

"Bill, it's too late. I can't. I'm so tired. I just want out."

It's not too late

Cases such as Ellie and Bill's are becoming more prevalent in my counseling experience. Sadly, there are almost as many Christian couples in this marital crisis as non-Christian. Twenty years ago, couples who walked into my office often said they came because of a specific problem or set of problems. Over the years, I've seen more and more couples who come to counseling after at least one partner has given up all hope for the marriage.

But there is hope for such a marriage. I have worked to help couples find joy in marriage for nearly thirty years. I can assure you that it is not too late.

Men, this book is written for you. It will give you insight into marital problems that often arise after several years and provide you with some biblical tools to correct those problems. Granted, there are different levels of marital problems. You may just be trying to keep your marriage healthy. You may be hearing the first knocks or funny sounds of trouble, or you may be on the verge of a complete breakdown in your relationship. At any of those stages, this book can aid you in communicating better with your spouse. The purpose of this book is to:

- Help you define trouble spots in your marriage and work through them together with your wife.

- Help you and your wife rediscover the love you may feel that you've lost.

- Help you and your wife reexamine the very foundation on which your marriage was based.

- Help you and your wife rediscover true commitment and romance in your marriage.

God's design

First, we will look to the author of love, God himself. The Bible tells us in John 4:7 that God is love. His love is unconditional. He continues to love us when we make mistakes, when we fail in our commitment to him, and even when we go days, weeks, or months without talking to him. In Genesis 2:18, 21–24, God reveals how he wants marriage partners to find fulfillment and contentment in one another:

> The LORD God said, "It is not good for the man to be alone. I will make a helper suitable for him."... So the LORD God caused the man to fall into a deep sleep; and while he was sleeping, he took one of the man's ribs and closed up the place with flesh. Then the LORD God made a woman from the rib he had taken out of the man, and he brought her to the man. The man said, "This is now bone of my bones and flesh of my flesh; she shall be called 'woman,' for she was taken out of man." For this reason a man will leave his father and mother and be united to his wife, and they will become one flesh.

The first man God created needed a companion. It was not just a desire, but a God-given need. God met that need by creating a woman, and Adam stated that Eve was "bone of my bones and flesh of my flesh." From the beginning, God ordained the concept of oneness in marriage. Man is to leave his father and mother—leave them, not just physically, but emotionally too. He is to leave behind the emotional, mental, and physical bonds that tie him closer to them than to any other. A new bond, a new life joined as one, begins with marriage. Before marriage, you are an integral part of a family unit. At marriage, you are still a part of your family, but a much stronger bond has been forged. The leaving and uniting in Genesis 2 describes a bonded relationship, like two pieces of paper being glued together. These pieces become one. It is impossible to pull them apart without

Marriage is not just a joining of your bodies but also a union of your mind, soul, and spirit.

tearing both pieces. This uniting symbolizes a perfect fit, one in which love can flourish. Marriage is not just a joining of your bodies but also a union of your mind, soul, and spirit.

This perfect fit requires love. But what do we mean by that four-letter word? We sometimes use it with great emotion ("I love you with all of my heart!") and sometimes with carelessness ("I love a good hot dog."). We apply this word to our wives, our children, our family, and our friends. Does it mean the same thing in all of these contexts?

The four facets of love

The New Testament uses four different words that we translate as love. Each word describes an aspect of the love relationship that is involved if you truly love your spouse as God designed in marriage. Let's briefly consider each of these Greek words to gain a better understanding of love:

- *eros*: sensual, passionate love

- *philéo*: feelings of friendship

- *storgé*: affection, as between parents and children

- *agapé*: a conscious action, beyond feelings, a chosen commitment

1. Eros
Your relationship with your wife probably began with the eros form of love. You were physically attracted to her when you first met, or you developed such an attraction to her over time. Most of us can recall spending an hour or two on the phone with our loved one, and that was after spending the entire evening with her. You didn't really have anything to say; you just wanted to hear her voice.

Walking with her in the snow in the reflected moonlight gave you all the warmth you needed. Making snow angels or stomping out "I love you" in the snow brought laughter and kisses. Simple tasks like making a dinner together seemed exciting and fun. Erotic love is like that. It may express itself in laughter, in looking deeply into your lover's eyes and melting, in emotional and physical fireworks. But just as fireworks light up the sky with brilliance and then fade away, so too can the excitement of *eros*. It must be nurtured with *philéo*, *storgé*, and finally *agapé*.

We will explore each of these facets of love throughout this book. But as you begin reading, I want you to ask yourself, "What kind of love is holding my marriage together?" Or, "What kind of love is missing in my marriage right now?" Each of the four kinds of love is needed to keep a marriage flourishing and growing. Too often, we get bogged down in just one aspect of love and neglect the others. Where are you? Is your marriage based primarily on eros? If it was based on physical intimacy in the beginning, have you also nurtured the other facets of your love?

2. Philéo

Have you become best friends or soul mates with your wife? Have you become so comfortable in your friendship that romance doesn't seem necessary? God created Eve to come alongside Adam. She was Adam's best and only friend besides God. But she was more, so much more. A woman wants to be your friend, your best friend. She wants to know you better than anyone on earth does. She needs the same from you. As wonderful as this *philéo* type of love is, you cannot build a marriage on that alone. Your wife also needs romance, and so do you. Men find satisfaction in the mating chase. The excitement of winning her attention, her love, and her adoration drew you together. You need the companionship of *philéo* as well as the excitement of *eros* in your marriage.

I see many marriages suffering because they're stuck in one of these two modes of love. The marriage is in neutral, not going anywhere. To be maintained, marital love must be renewed and nurtured to keep the relationship moving forward. Discontent comes when the marriage is just idling.

3. Storgé

We will deal further with the need for *eros* and *philéo* in the course of this book, but now I'd like to introduce the other two types of love, *storgé* and *agapé*, both of which are also vital to marriage. As you stood before your friends and relatives on your wedding day and gazed into each other's eyes, you made promises to love one another in sickness and in health, in prosperity and in poverty. Those were promises of *storgé* love. Many of us don't truly understand the depth and self-sacrifice of *storgé* love at the beginning. True, we wanted to give that kind of love to the person we adored, and we realized that we needed that type of love ourselves. But it is only over time, through joys and trials, that we can develop this type of deep commitment to our spouse.

Storgé love grows from and is nurtured by *philéo* and *eros*. It adds a deeper dimension to your love affair with your wife. It helps to bond those two pieces of paper together. It is the feeling you had as you looked up from your newborn baby and into the eyes of your tired yet radiant wife. Over time, some couples tend to take this deep affection for granted. It becomes such an intricate part of their relationship that it isn't recognized for the precious gift it is.

4. Agapé

Finally, there is *agapé*—the committed, unconditional love that defies all human logic. It is the type of love that says, "I will always love you, no matter what. I love you even though you're not making me happy right now. I love you for who you are."

Nothing can change *agapé* love because it is not based on what your wife does, how she makes you feel, or how she looks. It is not based on anything but her. If your love is based on anything other than who she is, then your love can fail when circumstances change.

By contrast, *agapé* love never fails. It is the unconditional love that Paul speaks of in Ephesians 5:25–33:

> Husbands, love your wives, just as Christ loved the church and gave himself up for her to make her holy, cleansing her by the washing with water through the word, and to present her to himself as a radiant church, without stain or wrinkle or any other blemish, but holy and blameless. In this same way, husbands ought to love their wives as their own bodies. He who loves his wife loves himself. After all, no one ever hated his own body, but he feeds and cares for it, just as Christ does the church—for we are members of his body. "For this reason a man will leave his father and mother and be united to his wife, and the two will become one flesh." This is a profound mystery—but I am talking about Christ and the church. However, each one of you also must love his wife as he loves himself, and the wife must respect her husband.

This scripture teaches you to put your wife's needs first. God knew this would not be easy, but his command is to love as he loves, and Christ loves us unconditionally. He gave up his home in heaven to come to earth for us. He became a human being for us. He suffered for us. He died for us. Your love for your wife must be rooted in Christ's selfless love.

Just as Christ demonstrated his love in action, so must we. God knew our masculine nature when he commanded us to love our wives as our own bodies. Most of us have no problem nourishing and cherishing ourselves. God knew that only by giving this kind of active, effective love to our wives will we achieve true joy in marriage. Sitting in idle can render a marriage inoperable.

I compare marriage to auto mechanics throughout this book; it's interesting how similar they are. When a couple comes to my office, the husband may treat marriage counseling much like taking a car to the shop. He may say things such as:

- "It's been running a little rough lately."
- "I really have no idea what's wrong, but fix it fast. I've got a lot to do."
- "She crashed it. I was just sitting in the passenger seat."
- "How much will it cost to fix? Maybe we should declare it a total loss."
- "I'm thinking of getting rid of it. Can anything be salvaged?"

My task is to help couples reconnect the bonds that have been strained through neglect. I try to help them discover facets of love that have been missing in their relationship. This can be very hard work, especially if one spouse has been feeling neglected or taken for granted. (Let's face it, guys, that partner usually is not the man!) I challenge the husband to look deep within his relationship with his wife and ask, "Do I share each of the four loves with my wife? Have I truly bonded with her physically, emotionally, and spiritually?" It takes all of these types of love to establish the kind of relationship that the Bible calls "one flesh."

However, I tell couples at the outset that an enduring marriage depends upon Christ's lordship over each partner's life. Do you have that kind of relationship with Christ? If not, there is no spiritual base upon which to build. Remember, marriage is a picture of Christ's love for his followers. Without a life rooted in Christ, it is hard to build a marriage that expresses *agapé* love for one another. So I ask you

> **I tell couples at the outset that an enduring marriage depends upon Christ's lordship over each partner's life.**

again, Is Christ the Lord of your life? Your answer will determine the outcome you can expect.

Sacrifice and commitment

Total commitment is needed for a successful marriage. The word *commitment* may make us feel uneasy because most of us have made commitments we'd rather not have. We're reminded of work meetings we're required to attend, financial contributions we feel obliged to make, or even social events that our wives say we're committed to attending. However, I'm talking about another type of commitment, one we might call "committed love." It is a commitment to love your wife as long as you live. It is a commitment that says, "I am here for you always, no matter what."

God's Word tells you to love your wife as Christ loved the church and "gave himself up for her" (Eph 5:25). Verse 26 says that Christ gave himself for the church so that he might make it holy. Verse 27 makes that purpose even more explicit: "to present her to himself as a radiant church, without stain or wrinkle or any other blemish, but holy and blameless." God's Word then makes this a command for Christian husbands: "In this same way, husbands ought to love their wives as their own bodies." When our wives see and feel this type of love, they will want a very close relationship with us. These verses speak primarily of Christ and his sacrificial love for the church, but they make clear that this same sacrificial love is necessary for a happy and successful marriage. The highest priority given to you as a Christian husband is your wife, whom you are to protect, honor, and keep holy. Total commitment and total sacrifice are required.

When I was in college, I worked at an auto garage for a time, changing tires, oil, batteries, and so forth. Every day, I observed men who brought their cars to the shop for scheduled maintenance. These men kept their cars in perfect working order. Every aspect of their engines was checked and maintained. The bodies of their cars were polished to a bright gleam. The tires were so clean that I wondered how these cars could have been driven on the same streets that I traveled. Often, these men had their wives with them as they waited, and it struck me even then that many of these men gave little attention to their wives. I saw only a glimpse into their marriages, but it was telling. I often noticed these men say a short, irritated word to the women they supposedly loved at least as much as their cars. Sometimes, hardly a word was spoken between them. As I looked at the neglected wife, I wondered what had happened to her gleam.

I've thought of this more as I've tried to help married couples over the years. These men all seemed to have a great capacity to care, to give attention to the things they really loved. They clearly knew that attention to details and regular maintenance truly matter. But they funneled all of this knowledge into inanimate objects. Their automobiles made them proud, and that is very important to us as men, but cars feel no love and have no eternal purpose.

Tell me, where are your priorities? Where are your energies concentrated? Does your wife know she is cherished and cared for beyond all else on earth?

Perhaps you feel coldness in your marriage because, instead of seeking God's will, you have been pursuing your own will. Ask yourself if you have let other priorities replace the priority of "one flesh" in your marriage. Sometimes couples allow careers, money, material things, or friends rob them of their first love. Even a carefully planned dream vacation can be divisive if it requires you to take extra hours from your wife and family for weeks or months beforehand. You may deceive yourself into believing that the vacation is for her and therefore worth the hours from home, but is it worth sacrificing your relationship? This can be true for the quest for a new home, car, or anything that puts a wedge in your relationship with your wife. The promise to obtain wonderful things for your wife is often an illusion, expressing your own desires and not your wife's. For example:

- I promise to pay off our debts and accumulate a nest egg for retirement by working eighty hours a week.

- I promise to build our dream home but then sit in front of my 50" plasma TV while my wife sits alone in another room.

- I promise to relax by playing golf every chance I get, regardless of my wife's needs or desires.

Too often, we cloak our real motivations with the protest, "I'm doing this for you, for the kids, for us!" Let's be honest: If we truly have servant hearts, our wives will see no selfish motives in our actions. Remember that Christ gave his all without expecting anything in return— not anything in return. Can this be said of you and me? Unfortunately, the answer is often no.

If we truly have servant hearts, our wives will see no selfish motives in our actions.

It begins with you

If you truly desire a change in your marriage, it must begin with you. Ask yourself:

- What is the true purpose of my marriage?

- How do I express all four types of love to my wife on a daily basis?

- How to I exemplify true commitment and sacrifice in my marriage?

Pray that God will guide your desires. Ask him to refocus your life on your commitment to Christ. Let him show you how to reaffirm your commitment to your wife.

Committed love enables a couple to act consistently as "one flesh" in the Lord. When you do, your wife will see and feel Christ's love in and through you. Christ's love will be expressed in your daily speech, actions, and attitudes toward her. Your wife will see that you want only the best for her. As she feels secure in your love, she will be able to respect you as her husband.

 Complete the Diagnostic Evaluation on the next page before continuing.

DIAGNOSTIC EVALUATION

Answer the following questions. Then ask your wife to evaluate your answers. This is time for an open and honest discussion of your marriage, not for hurtful criticism. It's okay if your partner disagrees with some of your answers. Look into your own heart and see what you need to change.

1. How does romantic love reveal itself in my marriage today?

2. How am I different romantically from the beginning of our relationship?

3. Is my relationship with my wife stuck in neutral, expressing itself in just one or two of the four types of love described in this chapter?

4. How do I show my commitment to my spouse on a daily basis?

5. How do I reveal my commitment to Christ in my daily life? Does my wife see this?

6. How is Christ revealed in my actions, words, and attitudes toward my wife?

2. REFOCUSING THE HEADLIGHTS

2. REFOCUSING THE HEADLIGHTS
KNOWING YOURSELF REQUIRES KNOWING GOD

"For now we see in a mirror dimly." —1 Corinthians 13:12 NASB

Bret, now in his late forties, sat in my office and said, "My wife and I have been married now for twenty-five years. We have been through deep waters and climbed some high mountains in our life, but she looks at me and says that she feels so alone. She says I do not know her, that I have not really tried to get to know her throughout all of these years. She states that she does not feel special anymore, that she has not felt special since the early part of our marriage. Dr. Vaughn, I have worked hard at being a good husband and provider for both her physical and emotional needs, but somehow I failed. I am not sure how to truly be emotional or intimate. I thought I did. For a long time I really thought I was doing it right, but I am not sure anymore. Apparently, I have failed."

Start with God

Wow! Have you ever thought or said this about yourself? We live in a day when psychology articulates, "Know thyself." Biblically, how can you know yourself without knowing, truly knowing, the God who created you? The psalmist states that God knows your innermost being, inside and outside, and reflects that God knew him even from his mother's womb. Each of us wants God to reveal the kind of person he wants us to be. We know God cannot work in our marriages until he works in our own lives. What might God need to change and possibly rebuild in your individual life for your marriage to become better? He might change your attitude, your behavior, your mood, or even your personality. In order to become open to your spouse and create positive changes in your marriage, real transformation must begin in you. Are you willing to allow God to reveal any problems in your personal life? Are you ready to accept what he reveals about your personal flaws, and resolve to change them?

Every self-help book starts by suggesting some formula about knowing yourself intimately. However, I believe this question must be addressed differently if you are a Christian. In a Christian's life, the self is dissolved in Christ, who works within you and changes you to be more like him. *The Purpose-Driven Life*, Rick Warren's popular book, begins with the stunning announcement: "It's not about you." As a Christian, within your marriage, your life is not about you but rather about meeting the needs of your marriage. This truth warrants deeper examination as we consider the relationship with our wives.

To love your spouse is to set aside your own needs as the first priority and to take on a servant's heart, as mentioned in the previous chapter. It means demonstrating a sacrificial love for the one you have married. This is the essence of true love, giving up yourself for your spouse. I'm not suggesting that a Christian husband must be a doormat. I do not believe that God requires you to lose your self-confidence or self-esteem, or have a poor self-image, in order to meet the needs of your spouse. But how will you need to change so that your spouse can have a deeper knowledge and respect for you and so that you can gain a deeper understanding of her personal needs and expectations?

Let's again look at Ephesians 5, as it gives us Christian men very clear direction about how we should love our wives. It states that we are to love our wives as Christ loved the church. How does one accomplish this? Christ did it by giving himself for the church.

He gave his entire life for us. So we are called first of all to give up everything for our wives.

Today's culture focuses on the need to love yourself. Pop psychology says that if you care for your own needs and desires first, then somehow you will be able to understand and love the person you are involved with. This is a belief that commonly arises when many people think about divorce or separation. They say, "I need [or deserve] to be happy." Interestingly, there is no place in Scripture that states that happiness is our highest priority in marriage. In fact, God's Word focuses on contentment and that contentment can emerge within our lives when we love someone else more than ourselves. God wants us to be balanced by being other-focused.

For the Christian, knowing yourself means losing yourself in Christ; it means becoming less of yourself and more of Christ. Galatians 2:20 states, "I have been crucified with Christ and I no longer live, but Christ lives in me. The life I live in the body, I live by faith in the Son of God, who loved me and gave himself for me." So often I will hear a wife say, "Dr. Vaughn, he just changed. He is not the man I married." Sometimes I will hear the husband say, "I do not know her anymore. It seems as if the woman I married just left." Does any of this sound familiar? It is quite possible for a person to change, even a Christian. The center of a person's life may shift from self to Christ, or it may shift the other way. A Christian should be remolded in the image of Christ. A true servant with a true servant's heart will direct his energy toward meeting the needs of his or her spouse rather than meeting the individual's own needs. If that was once true and has changed, it means we really are dealing with a different person. The marriage cannot be transformed until the marriage partners are individually transformed into the likeness of Christ.

Attitude adjustment

In my office sits a large, wooden-handled mallet made from rough wood. On the side of the mallet are two words: *Attitude Adjuster*.

In the course of a marriage, each partner occasionally needs an attitude adjustment. Proverbs 23:7 says as a man "thinks in his heart, so is he" (NKJV). The Bible uses the term *heart* to refer to the deepest part of your being, which drives and motivates you to act and respond in various ways to others. Your heart is what ultimately charts your life's direction. When Christ came into your life, did he change your heart and set a new course for your life, or did he simply modify the course you had chosen for yourself? If your answer is, "He modified my life," it's likely that you do not see the need for trying to change your life now. You probably see no need to be more understanding of your spouse.

Rather, you're likely to wonder, "Why do I have to change my attitude? Why does it always have to be me? Why can't it be her?" The argument that I often hear in counseling is, "I have done enough changing. It is time for her to change. It's my turn to see changes in my wife." Marriage partners often set themselves up for this. Many times during courtship, problems or concerns will arise and the lovers say to themselves, "It is not that big of an issue. Besides, when we are married, all that will change." After marriage, they ask, "Why won't my spouse change? I thought he or she would definitely change when we got married."

Marital unhappiness is not necessarily rooted in poor communication. More often, it arises from preconceived expectations of what marriage should be. One or both partners bring baggage from previous relationships that they expect the new relationship to handle. They believe the spouse will fix the problems of their past.

Again, let's reflect back on Ephesians 5. The Bible tells us to love sacrificially, adjusting to our wives' needs. As we do this, our wives will feel secure and safe, allowing them to reflect true love in return. As we connect to our wives' needs, we build commitment and a solid foundation that they can trust. We establish an openness that feels comfortable. That sacrificial love will be returned with the sincere and honest respect that every husband desires.

Personality shift

Look into a mirror and ask yourself the following questions: (1) Am I a negative person? Do I show a negative attitude in how I view my marriage, my life, or life situations in general? (2) Do I often blame other people for problems? Do I shift responsibility for problems to others, specifically my spouse? These are hard questions to answer because none of us like to believe such things about ourselves. However, let's take a look at the implication these problems have for a marriage.

If the base of your marriage is to be solid, you may need to make some significant shifts in your own foundational attitudes, priorities, and life goals. We refer to the combination of these things as your personality. Yes, I'm actually suggesting that your personality may need to change—and the Bible says it can change.

I often hear people in counseling sessions playing "old tapes" about the past. The old tapes reflect childhood or adolescent relationships with family and friends. There may be nothing wrong here, unless those old tapes are faulty or built upon expectations that no longer exist. Maybe you are thinking, "Okay, here is where my parents are to blame, right?" or, "This is the reason that I act the way I do today." No, I am not talking about fault-finding. On the contrary, I think you need to understand what your old tapes are saying. Maybe they are constructive, maybe not. But only when you understand these old tapes will you understand how your own self-view needs to be changed.

Old tapes that do not work may stop you from having a servant's heart. They can prevent you from manifesting true love for your spouse.

> So God changes our thinking, "renews our minds," to change our relationships.

This is where God starts. He changes our behaviors and eliminates old patterns so that we begin to reflect God's design and his love. God's Word is clear that our thinking affects the way we relate to the world around us. So God changes our thinking, "renews our minds," to change our relationships. If you evaluate your customary patterns of behavior and thought, you may gain new insight about how you need to change your speech and behavior. This personality shift can bring change in your marriage.

I often hear people reflect that they married someone in character like their mother or father. They looked for characteristics they saw in their parents, whom they saw as healthy human beings while growing up. So, it was not unusual to desire those same traits in a spouse.

However, the characteristics that attract you at the beginning of your relationship may later push you away from the same person. Your spouse is often unaware that he or she is being graded on your parent's terms and is not able to measure up to what you expected him or her to be. Remember, you may have assumed at the beginning of a relationship that you could change the person after you were married, but this rarely ever happens. I see many couples who truly believed that after marriage they could enhance the "good" traits of their spouse and eliminate the "bad" traits. When those changes do not materialize, resentment and bitterness are the result.

Exactly what changes do you want your wife to make? Are you hoping to change your wife? If this is the case, then resentment and bitterness have already started and probably have led to a certain amount of emotional detachment from your spouse. Do you expect God to change you or your wife first? Do you pray that God will reveal what needs to be changed in your life and attitude in order to rebuild your marriage? How often are sarcastic words, put-downs, and personal digs a part of your conversations with your wife? Do you try to manipulate her emotions? These are questions you must ask yourself.

A change in your very personality may be required if change in your marriage is to be real and lasting. Begin by asking God to show you what will be required in order for your marriage to become one of contentment and peace. Seek to invite him into your life like never before, breaking down any strongholds in yourself in order to make you a new creation for your spouse. I know these are difficult requests. However, you need to address any barriers in your own life that prevent Christ from truly living within you in order to have the spiritual walk that you desire with your mate. Your ultimate goal is to have life in which your spouse will feel uplifted by you each day. This does not require a holier-than-thou attitude but rather a servant's heart that seeks to meet the needs of your spouse. The change starts with you, not with your wife.

Romans 9:20–21 speaks of God's molding us like a potter molds a lump of clay. God created each of us for a special purpose. We must let him continue to mold us daily to fit the tasks he has given us. He can transform us so that we will be more like him each day. When we allow him to do that, we can be sufficient for all areas of marriage.

Focus on the basics

Remember, you cannot build a sound structure on a faulty foundation. You need to start with the very foundation of your Christian life if you are to erect a sound marriage. For this reason, the next few pages may seem very simplistic; however, your foundation must be firm if you are going to become the man your spouse deserves. You may want to bypass the basics so you can begin working on the new and improved model of your marriage, but let me share a secret: There can be no new and improved model until you have mastered the basics of mature Christian living. So, let's embark on a refresher course in what is really important in your life as a Christian man.

God's Word
When challenges come to a marriage, it's easy to let our emotions dictate our thoughts and behavior. However, emotions are fickle

and changeable. You cannot build a stable foundation on something that is constantly shifting. Several years ago, Dr. James Dobson published a book, *Emotions: Can You Trust Them?*, in which he warns us to be wary of feelings because they can be easily manipulated and swayed in wrong directions. It is interesting to note in the Gospels that Christ did not focus on emotions in his conversations with his disciples. He focused on the eternal truths of God. For this reason, God's Word is a reliable guide for your marriage. How often do you pick up the Bible to seek God's direction for your life?

A common joke is that we men do not stop and ask for directions when we're traveling. Unfortunately, that's often true. Our masculine pride makes us think we are fine, we know where we are going and we do not need anyone's help to reach our destination. We don't want to admit it, but we allow our pride to take control. At other times, it may be fear, insecurity, or just plain stubbornness! Our fear of not knowing or being wrong compels us to keep on driving, refusing to stop and ask questions, even though we're unsure of our course. We reassure ourselves that it will all work out and that in the end it will all come together. Sometimes that's true, sometimes not.

God gave us his Word to guide our personal lives, and that includes our marriages. When we allow business activities and other priorities to pull us away from God's Word, we lose his direction. Ask yourself the following two questions:

1. When was the last time you stopped and read God's Word because you wanted God's direction for an important decision in your life?

2. When was the last time you read God's Word for any reason, on your own, for more than fifteen minutes?

I am amazed in counseling sessions to discover how many couples say that God is supremely important in their lives but their actions do not match their words. They will tell me that they spent time reading and studying God's Word together when they were dating, yet that practice is gone or has greatly diminished since they were married. The failure to study God's "road map" regularly tricks you into trusting yourself and not God for life's answers. The psalmist states that God's Word is a light to my path and that I must hide his Word in my heart to stay focused in the right direction (Ps 119:105, 11). If you do this, you will be able to follow God's direction for your life and your spouse's, not a self-willed direction. Did you start your marriage with God in mind? Is he at the foundation of who you are now or only a showpiece to impress your spouse? If you leave God's Word on the shelf, you travel without the road map God provided to keep you on course. Your spiritual connection with him will be broken.

Throughout my career, I have had the opportunity to teach several college courses. I have observed that some college students want good grades but are not willing to put forth the effort needed to obtain those grades. When test time comes and the grade is disappointing, they assure me that they did read and study the material. After some prompting, the truth usually comes out. They say something like, "OK, Dr. Vaughn, I should have studied a little bit more. But there were so many other important things taking up my time!" The poor grade reveals their lack of preparedness. There is no escaping the fact that we must prepare to obtain satisfactory results.

Tests will come to your marriage as well. Busy times will come. If God's Word is not a priority in the busy times, the results of your tests will fall far short of what you expected for your marriage. How can anyone be a spiritual leader, even in a marriage, if he is a below-average student of the Master's life plan? Your marriage partner deserves the best you can give her. Letting God's Word permeate your life will enable you to give her the best. Couples in counseling often say they would give anything for just a hint that God is working in their spouse's life. If you were both committed Christians while dating, don't drift into complacency or complete disregard for God's Word.

Do any of these points seem familiar? If your marriage has drift-ed away from God, the question must be asked: Who changed—you, your wife, or both of you? You may want to defend yourself at this juncture. We men can easily use the excuse that work, financial obligations, and the raising of our kids require so much of us that there is just no time for studying the Bible. But there is time. It must be a matter of priority. Your marriage will not last unless you renew your reliance on your Creator each day. That begins with the study of Scripture.

Prayer and meditation

"I remember when we used to sit and pray together about our future," Jill stated to me. "I felt so close to him. I was committed to him. He would talk to me about how God was working in his life, and I felt like we were becoming one. I thought how great it was that I had this man in my life who wanted to be close to God and close to me with God."

Tears began to run down Jill's face as she continued. "Then… I don't know. After we were married, it just seemed to stop. We would still pray at dinner, but that just seemed trivial. When I would ask him about the change, it seemed to annoy him, so I just stopped asking. Now God and prayer seem so distant. I just wish things could be back to where they were in the beginning."

Jill's words reveal another piece of a broken foundation in her mar-riage, another key to touching her heart. The regular practice of praying together is an important way of touching God each day and letting her see this in your actions. Prayer opens up a connec-tion directly to God. It builds and strengthens us when the storms of life blow our way. Unfortunately, prayer can become another casualty of our busy schedules if not kept as a priority. You may say that you did take time to pray together at the beginning of your relationship, but now too many obstacles get in the way. Remem-ber this: praying with your spouse can have no depth unless your own prayer life with God is healthy. This may seem basic, but it is necessary if you are going to reestablish a solid prayer life with your marriage partner. A triad diagram illustrates what I'm saying. Your relationship with God at the top will become better connected as each of you move toward God.

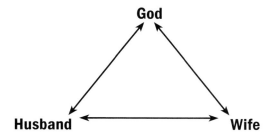

Likewise, the closer you move to God in your actions and thoughts, the closer you move toward your partner. Of course, this assumes that your partner is also willing to move closer to God. Outside of sexual relations, you will find no closer intimacy with your spouse than spiritual intimacy, which is what God intended. As both of you open up to God, he opens up to you. This vulnerability to God creates an openness for you as a couple, allowing for deeper communication and moments of intimate sharing together. Your spouse needs to see God working in your life. This means you need to make time to reconnect with God in your own life. Time of solitude talking with God can lead to spiritual renewal and refocusing on his guidance to help you in life's daily struggles. In Isaiah 1:18, God says that he desires to spend time with you reasoning together. To be a true reflection of God to your spouse, you must communicate directly and openly with the master Teacher. Such times of quiet meditation with God will allow you to lay your fears and anxieties at the Master's feet and let him renew his peace within you. First Peter 5:7 says you can place all of your cares on him and he alone will take care of you.

Married couples often tell me that it is difficult for them to pray aloud with one another. That's okay. Taking time to be together, even in silent prayer, can open up a connection between the two of you and with the Father himself. You do not have to be articulate in your praying. Prayer is just talking with God. That is the beauty of prayer. It is just sharing with God our everyday needs, problems, and concerns. Intimacy will grow between both of you in those times of sharing together with God. Couples often describe how a daily time of prayer together has established a bond between them that they have not experienced in any other fashion.

Couples have also told me how sharing a verse of Scripture with their spouse, or sharing a thought that came to them during their private meditations with God, has created a newness in their relationship that they continue to desire.

We often assume that meditation is an intense and highly disciplined experience. However, meditation is nothing more than taking time to process, replay, and refocus on what God is showing you in your day-to-day journey. My wife and I sometimes take a verse of Scripture and think on that verse throughout the day, sometimes even over a few days, and then share with each other how God has used that verse in our experience. The book of Joshua says that the families of Israel were to meditate on God's Word day and night; they were not to let God's Word depart from their speech. Why? Because then they would "be prosperous and successful" (Josh 1:8). Do you want a successful and prosperous family life and marriage? Then you need to be immersed in God's Word. God alone can establish and maintain the strong connection that you need with your marriage partner. To be spiritually fed, you must take time daily to be alone with God. Then spend time together with your spouse in conversation with God so that together you can make the foundation of your marriage solid again.

You are ready to rebuild your marriage when these foundational steps of reading God's Word and praying together are in place. Your relationship with God must be maintained differently this time—much differently—if you are to be bound together in divine love. You do not want to come back this way again, so it is important to keep on following God's road map.

 Complete the Diagnostic Evaluation on the next page before continuing.

DIAGNOSTIC EVALUATION

Meditate on these questions together as a couple:

1. How do you see God working to strengthen your marriage?

2. Do you both believe that God's Word is the blueprint for your personal life and your marriage? If so, how often do you spend time together in prayer and the study of his Word?

3. How is your life with your spouse and family different than it might have been because of your faith in God?

4. Does your spouse see evidence of God in you when both of you seek direction for your marriage, including the problems that arise?

5. Do you find strength and renewal for your marriage when spending time with God? If not, what has changed?

3. CLEARING THE ERROR CODES

3. CLEARING THE ERROR CODES
LEARNING THE ART OF FORGIVENESS

"Forgiveness is a beautiful word, until you have something to forgive." —C. S. Lewis

"I do not know if I can ever forgive her for the pain that she has caused me," John said. "So many terrible, awful things she has done to me. Now, because she is sorry, I am just supposed to forgive all of this and go on as if nothing ever happened. I do not think so. It is not that easy. I am never going to be hurt like this again. Never! Do you understand me? Never again!"

Susan, now in tears, responded, "I know I was very wrong. I really am sorry. I do not know why I did such terrible things, but I am trying to change, John. I really am. What can I do to show you how sorry I am? I want our marriage to work. I want to be with you. Please, can't we try again?

The basis for forgiveness

Moral failure, emotional abuse, or even physical abuse will tear at the very core of a marriage relationship. Forgiveness can be most difficult in such circumstances. A marriage enveloped by deceit and dishonesty cannot move forward until true forgiveness occurs. Two questions are often asked:

1. Why should I ask for forgiveness?

2. Why should I forgive after so much hurt was done to me?

These two very complicated questions often appear in marital counseling. To answer them, we must return to the foundation of forgiveness provided in God's Word. Ephesians 4:31–32 says,

> Get rid of all bitterness, rage and anger, brawling and slander, along with every form of malice. Be kind and compassionate to one another, forgiving each other, just as in Christ God forgave you.

These powerful words were written in order to create change within a community of Christians, but they are just as applicable to a Christian husband and wife. Ephesians 5:1 goes on to say, "Be imitators of God, therefore, as dearly loved children." The phrase, "imitators of God" means that we Christians are to be like God. So here are two more tough questions for a Christian couple who are experiencing deep pain in their relationship:

1. When you have been deeply hurt or mistreated, does your spouse deserve forgiveness for what he or she has done to you?

2. Does your spouse need to feel some type of remorse for what he or she has done to you before you would even consider forgiveness?

Most often, individuals say they will not consider offering forgiveness to their marriage partner until that partner understands the pain that she or he has inflicted. Let's return again to scripture to see the basis of its exhortation to forgive. If we turn backward a couple of chapters in Paul's letter to the Ephesians, we find this:

But because of his great love for us, God, who is rich in mercy, made us alive with Christ even when we were dead in transgressions—it is by grace you have been saved.

God gives us grace. Grace is something we are freely given, although we do not deserve it. God provided grace to each one of us, even when we deserved no grace at all. You may be saying that you are not God and that the pain that you feel is too great to extend forgiveness to the person who hurt you. How are you supposed to give someone gracious forgiveness when your trust and security have been so badly damaged?

Forgiveness is often withheld when infidelity has taken place. Hurt and resentment are so great that the injured spouse may believe that forgiveness is impossible. However, forgiveness cannot be granted by you alone. God himself will need to extend forgiveness through you to your spouse in this situation. Forgiveness can be defined as releasing or freeing a person from a debt. The offense is totally removed from the relationship, never to be held against the offender again. Humanly, we cannot do this, but with God all things are possible. So if your spouse has been unfaithful to you, forgiveness is not only necessary—it is possible.

> **Forgiveness can be defined as releasing or freeing a person from a debt. The offense is totally removed from the relationship.**

Taking stock

To begin moving toward forgiveness, I believe you need to take four steps:

1. Take inventory of your part in the problem created.

2. Consider what you need to do because of your contribution to the problem.

3. Recognize your ability through Christ to release your spouse from any bitterness or resentment that the problem has created in your relationship.

4. Acknowledge that your spouse needs unconditional forgiveness in order to restore your relationship. Your spouse does not need a second chance, marital probation, or leniency; your spouse needs unconditional forgiveness.

I often counsel with offended marriage partners who are willing to admit that they bear some responsibility for what happened. They recognize that they need to change, even that they need to make some sort of apology for their own failures. But they insist that their spouses must bear some type of punishment or undergo some sort of discipline for what they have done. (That's called retribution.) Until the offenders do that, the "victims" are not willing to forgive. Here is the tough part of forgiveness: It means releasing the offender from all consequences. It means putting away the pain and the memory of that pain forever. It means not bringing the incident back to their account in later years, whatever the offense might have been.

Forgiveness and forgetting

Of course, there remains the issue of forgiving versus forgetting. We know that forgiving and forgetting are different facets of the process, but they are in fact linked together. Forgiving injustice takes time and is a component if you are to move forward in your marriage when you have been wronged. However, Scripture specifically urges us to imitate Christ in the way we forgive anyone who wrongs us: Christ forgives and puts away our transgressions, *not remembering them or bringing them against us again* (see Heb 8:12;

10:17). His forgiveness is complete and final. We have the ability to do that too, because he lives in us. When our marriage partner has wronged us, we can forgive our spouse of wrongdoing and forget the wrongdoing because of God's love working in us. That must become our priority.

Several years ago, I counseled with a young couple who were going through significant marital problems because of unresolved resentment and lack of forgiveness for past offenses. Molly said their problems were very serious, due to Ted's lack of attentiveness and sincerity. In one particular session, Molly became furious with Ted. She complained that Ted was insensitive, lacked a caring and compassionate spirit, and did not recognize her emotional needs. I asked if she could give some examples of this so that Ted would better understand what type of behavior was hurting her. "Well, Dr. Vaughn, I will have to take you back to the beginning of our marriage to explain why it is so painful," she said. "I cannot forgive Ted for almost killing me."

Of course, this statement changed everything in the counseling session. I looked at Ted and began, "Ted, this is a very serious accusation. Can you explain what Molly is saying?"

Realizing that he was in deep trouble, he turned to Molly and said, "I am sorry for anything and everything I have done to hurt you. I love you, Molly. Please forgive me. I beg you to forgive me for whatever I did that almost killed you."

Molly was unimpressed. "That is not going to cut it, Ted," she responded. "It will not fix it this time."

Molly, with as much intensity as I have ever seen in a counseling session, looked straight at Ted and said, "No forgiveness. Not until you explain to Dr. Vaughn and to me how your insensitive attitude almost killed me and our baby." Now it was not just Molly who had almost been killed but also their baby!

Ted's expression looked like the proverbial "deer in headlights." It was obvious that he was trying frantically to recall what he did that nearly killed Molly and their baby. He began, "Baby, we only have one son, and he is nine years old. How did I almost kill you and him? I have no clue what you're talking about."

Molly turned to me and said, "See, Dr. Vaughn? This is exactly what I have been talking about. Can you believe that this guy does not even remember something as important as this? What kind of man would forget such a traumatic event?" Turning back to Ted, she sneered, "And you want forgiveness?"

After a few moments, Molly regained her composure and I asked her to tell me exactly what had happened. She said that nine years previously, she had been pregnant with their son as they were building a new home. On the day that the concrete driveway was to be poured, Ted was busy setting up the forms for the sidewalks and driveway. He had been trying to do much of the work himself in order to save money. By the time the concrete truck arrived, it had begun to rain hard. Molly said that she came outside at one point, as the rain was pouring down, and tried to get Ted's help with a problem inside the house. She stated that she knew Ted was stressed but still should have noticed her cries for help. At the same moment, one of the forms broke and concrete began spilling onto the ground. In frustration, Ted threw a shovel in her direction. As she remembered the incident, the shovel landed right at her feet. She retreated into the house, crying because of the danger that Ted had placed her and the baby in.

At this point, Ted looked totally bewildered. He said, "I don't remember throwing the shovel, let alone throwing it toward you, Molly. Everything was going wrong that day. It seemed as though I could not do anything right. I am sorry, truly sorry, for whatever I did and how you perceived it. I would have never done anything to hurt you or the baby."

He paused and then added, "Molly, that was nine years ago. You have held onto this for nine years?"

That incident was not the only reason that Ted and Molly had come for counseling, but the lack of forgiveness had created a bitterness that led to other problems nine years later. If forgiveness is not given or expressed, the resulting pain and resentment can destroy the very structure of a marital relationship. Forgiveness is truly a choice, our choice. We must choose to release our spouses from the debts they owe us if our marriages are to grow and thrive. Throughout your marriage, there will be many times when you will have to ask God to enable you to forgive an injustice that your marriage partner has done to you, even though it has created tremendous emotional and possibly even physical pain. Only God himself can give you the peace your relationship will need to overcome these situations. Isaiah 26:3 clearly states that God will give us perfect peace, but we must remain focused on him to receive it.

> **We must choose to release our spouses from the debts they owe us if our marriages are to grow and thrive.**

Focusing upon God's love and letting God work through you are essential to forgiveness. Only through God can you find the forgiveness and peace for your marriage that allow healing to take place.

Forgiveness requires more than just a change of heart and attitude; it requires a change in your behavior. Left unchanged, hurtful behavior patterns lead to bitterness. If you want to be reconciled to your spouse, you will actively seek change in your own behaviors and actions. When you ask God to create in you a new heart, you are also asking him to motivate new actions and inspire a new way of thinking within you. These changes will allow your spouse to see a new direction in your life, not only hear it in your words.

Forgiveness leads to restoration

A fundamental issue related to forgiveness that also needs attention is the matter of restoration. Restoration means bringing your marital relationship back to its former place, making it new again. Restoration is rebuilding your marriage, not abandoning it.

Divorce is not restoration. Many couples believe that divorce is the only way to escape the hurt and humiliation that they may have endured. In some ways, restoration is more difficult than divorce, yet restoration is the best answer to a breakdown in your marriage. It's the way God would have you proceed when serious marital problems arise. I know that it may seem impossible to think about restoring your relationship with your spouse, especially if your spouse has engaged in adultery, lying, or deceit. However, even in these circumstances, it is possible to make your marriage new again.

You may ask, "Doesn't God allow divorce in certain situations?" The answer is yes. However, his ultimate goal was never for divorce to be the answer to marital problems. When we exchange marriage vows, we talk about becoming "one body." God said, "For this reason a man will leave his father and mother and be united to his wife, and they will become one flesh" (Gen 2:24). I have seen the pain and agony brought about by marital unfaithfulness. It is a crushing blow to a marriage. It seems insurmountable. However, Scripture urges all Christians—including Christian spouses—to "confess your sins to each other and pray for each other so that you may be healed" (James 5:16). Focus on the last few words of this verse: "so that you may be healed." Forgiveness brings healing. Restoration brings rebirth.

An unwillingness to forgive is like a cancer that spreads into all areas of your life. The bitterness that follows will take control of your life, leading you to shut out other persons and refuse to trust them. Bitter, resentful persons also shut God out of their lives because they feel deceived by him as well. The Bible clearly states that if I harbor any type of unbelief in my own heart, it prevents God from lifting me out of my pain (see Matt 13:57–58). By allowing God back into your painful heart and mind, healing will take place and restoration can begin. This process

By allowing God back into your painful heart and mind, healing will take place and restoration can begin.

takes time. Do not quit too soon or feel that it is useless. God alone knows the pain you are experiencing; he alone can remove the bitterness and restore in you a new spirit to love your spouse.

It is often easier to blame God than to seek his help when problems arise in our marriages. Christians often say things such as "God should have stopped this" or "God should have protected me from this." However, 1 Timothy 1:12 states, "I thank Christ Jesus our Lord, who has given me strength, that he considered me faithful, appointing me to his service." In other words, the Christian way is often difficult and full of potholes, but we need to remember that Christ set us on this way for good reason. The Lord is faithful to you, even when your marital road appears to be washed away with troubles and events that run contrary to anything you have imagined. He can enable you and your partner to go through these troubles so you both will be victorious. The key verse to remember is, "I will never leave you nor forsake you" (Josh 1:5; but see Deut 31:07–18). Your marriage will be restored if both of you are willing, through God, to be set free together from the past.

At times, you may believe that your journey to restoration is hopeless and your marital situation can never be changed. However, by forgiving your spouse, you not only release him or her from bondage, but you also set yourself free from the shackles holding you in the pain of your past. The results of restoration are joy, peace, and becoming one spirit again. God himself will knit your marriage together if you allow him. This will happen if you focus on him and allow him to renew your heart and mind. It is possible to begin even now, when you are questioning whether it's possible. God is the God of the impossible. Put your trust in him and him alone.

 Complete the Diagnostic Evaluation on the next page before continuing.

DIAGNOSTIC EVALUATION

Men, here are some tough questions that you will need to evaluate on your own:

1. Have I truly sought God's help concerning forgiveness for my wife and the relational problems we face?

2. Have I asked God to reveal to me my own role in the problems we have?

3. Can I accept what God reveals to me concerning the wrongs that I have committed and what I must do to bring about positive change?

4. Have I confronted the issues appropriately and biblically, seeking God first for his wisdom?

5. Is my wife ready to receive my forgiveness, and am I ready to forgive her freely?

6. Once confronted, do I seek restoration or do I seek retribution?

7. Is my attitude helping or hindering the restoration of my marriage? Are my actions and behavior different, showing a complete change of heart?

4. OVERHAULING THE ENGINE

4. OVERHAULING THE ENGINE
SECURING YOUR MARRIAGE
WITH TRUST, SECURITY, RESPECT

"And I show you a still more excellent way."
—1 Corinthians 12:31 NASB

Premarital counseling is a valuable tool, though it is seldom used by couples. Many consider it to be simply a checklist of issues to consider before getting married. Most couples believe they do not need premarital counseling because they know they were meant for each other. No need to waste time considering a question you have already answered!

I am not saying this simply because I am a professional psychologist but because I've seen it proven again and again: Many precious and wonderful insights come while you are engaged to be married. Taking time to understand what you will need to sustain your relationship and marriage is vital. A sound structure must be in place for your marriage to endure throughout the years.

I believe that your marriage will remain solid if you build it on three values. To use our automotive analogy, we could call these the engine mounts of your marriage because they give you the strength to withstand the shocks of life that will surely come to the two of you. These three stabilizing values are trust, security, and respect.

Trust

Trust should have characterized your relationship since the beginning, but sometimes it is not as solid as it needs to be as you proceed through life together. If that's true, let's consider how to strengthen your trust for one another. This is important not only for engaged couples but also for those who have been married for decades.

"Of course I trust him. He is the most wonderful man in the world!" Mary states. "Why would I question his trust? He is perfect!"

Don't laugh! You may have heard this at beginning of your relationship. In fact, you may agree that your partner can trust you because there's no reason for her not to trust. But what is trust? How have you established and maintained it in your relationship?

Trust could be defined as the belief in, and reliance on, the integrity of someone else. In a healthy marriage, you should be able to trust your partner with your emotional, physical and spiritual well-being. You want to be confident of your ability to trust your partner. You want your trust to be a sure thing. Trust is possible if both of you have a personal interest in keeping at the forefront of your attention the other person's needs and expectations of the relationship. Ephesians 5:22–20 reveals that building trust is the responsibility of men first as we practice loving our wives. You will recall that this passage refers to how Christ loved the church totally, giving his all for his followers. We men are to love our wives with the same wholehearted commitment that Christ had for the church. Trust is established not only by our words but also by our consistently loving actions. Our behavior toward our partners should be steady, readily evident, and unwavering over time. What you said to your spouse while dating must continue to be said—and demonstrated—if her trust is to be secure. This assumes, of course, that what you said was true and not just a line.

> **Building trust is the responsibility of men first as we practice loving our wives.**

Think again about the statements that are typically made at the beginning of a courtship: "He is just so wonderful." "She is the greatest woman on earth." "There is no one quite like you." These are tall orders to fill. However, reflect on what you said about one another and how those statements laid the foundation of trust in your relationship. Did you trust each other in ways that allowed you to be open and vulnerable to one another? Did you feel that your mate had your best interests at heart and truly understood what your heart's desires were? Were his or her actions consistent in building a caring and sincere relationship? Did you feel emotionally secure enough to express yourself openly with your partner? Many times, I will hear couples say they were "hoping and praying" that trust would emerge in their relationship. Somehow, trust was supposed to just be there, even if it was not evident while dating.

Unnecessary stress factors or questionable actions at the beginning of a relationship are oftentimes overlooked or even denied. Your emotional state ("This feeling is so wonderful!") may have kept you from seeing that a sound basis for trust was not present. Or you may have hoped and believed that somehow your relationship would develop trust. Denial may have covered pain and hurt that you experienced in the early days of the relationship. Later, however, this breakdown in trust can manifest itself in emotional pain that continues to grow. If these words describe what you have experienced in your marriage, you no doubt have little trust for one another presently. Sharing your emotions with your spouse will seem impossible. Over the course of time, without the underpinning of genuine trust in your relationship, the division between the two of you will become greater.

Remember, trust may be lost in numerous ways. Often, it is destroyed by a number of unresolved little issues; promises not kept or words inappropriately said can destroy the bond of trust. Trust can be rebuilt, but it depends on whether the two of you are willing to take the initiative to understand why your trust for one another collapsed. You both must take responsibility for the part you have played in this breakdown and be willing to do whatever it takes to restore trust.

How do you reestablish trust in your marriage if you lose it? Regardless of how trust is lost, we will focus first upon what you can do before we ask the question of your spouse. As the husband, you can take specific actions and adopt specific attitudes to enhance trust in your relationship.

The influence of the past

If your life is more self-centered than God-centered, you may find yourself constantly wondering about or questioning your spouse's behavior and actions without any real cause. If that's true, think about why you feel such insecurity, lack of intimacy, and vulnerability. Has anything happened in your past that may contribute to your lack of trust and your reluctance to be vulnerable to someone else?

> **If your life is more self-centered than God-centered, you may find yourself constantly wondering about or questioning your spouse's behavior.**

I'm not assuming that you have unresolved issues from your past, but if you have a history of unresolved family problems, that can be an important factor in your inability to trust your mate. If you experienced abuse, lack of nurturing, or neglect by your parents while growing up, that can diminish your ability to trust others even today. If you grew up in a family where trust was not evident, especially if trust was not seen in the relationship between your parents, you may have had no model to teach you how to be open with others. If such things were true of your past, you may seek an extra degree of validation before you trust anything or anyone. In fact, you may not trust anyone except yourself. Suspicion and constant questioning becomes your mode of operation. You read between the lines of what your spouse does or does not say. You project your own fears, anxieties, or false assumptions on your spouse, which prompts you to make accusations with no basis in your present reality; they are simply reflections of the mistrust you learned in your past.

For example, Becky sat in my office saying, "Dr. Vaughn, I do want to trust my husband. He has so many characteristics like my father that I never saw while we were dating." Becky's father drank heavily and "ran around" on her mother. Becky's mother often said that she could not trust Becky's father, and she had good reason, yet she never confronted him. "She would only talk to my brother and me about how bad our father was and how miserable she was," Becky explained. "I can remember how often she would tell me, 'You cannot trust any man, any of them. You must always watch out for yourself so that you don't end up like me.'"

You may feel that Becky's situation is very different from yours because your upbringing was not that bad. However, if trust is not established early in life, the tendency to mistrust other people will keep on playing like old tapes later. These old tapes interpret the new relationships that we are involved in today. Our marriages will be directly impacted by those old tapes.

The problem of unresolved guilt

Unresolved guilt from previous relationships can also create major trust problems and concerns in a marriage. I have counseled many individuals who feel unworthy of happiness and love because of their past actions. They are afraid to accept and reach out to establish trust with another member of the opposite sex, either before or after marriage. They are fearful that problems from their past may resurface to undermine new relationship. So often, these individuals come to counseling because they were committed to establishing a good marriage, but unresolved issues from previous relationships have crept in. Old relationships have begun to haunt their present marriage relationship. As one individual said, "It is as if the sins of my past return to my conscience, robbing me of the trust that I was hoping for and the contentment I need."

This unresolved guilt is most commonly felt because of sexual encounters and behaviors of the past. If you were involved in sexual improprieties in the past and now have feelings of inadequacy and shame, it is time to deal with the past. Until you do, your past will continue to complicate your relationship with your spouse, especially when you are trying to establish intimacy and trust. Women specifically tell me how they gave their bodies to men when they were younger in order to feel loved, only to be hurt and rejected again and again. They were looking for someone they believed they could trust, someone who would protect them and bring emotional stability to their lives, only to be rejected and abandoned when the sexual encounter was over.

However, men fall into these traps as well. I counseled one young man who had been raised in an alcoholic home and was sexually fondled by a cousin throughout his childhood. He grew up believing he needed to grant sexual favors in order to receive love. He thought that sexual activity "would get me what I needed." He trusted no one, but he constantly hoped the right woman would come along and change his life. Throughout college, he had recreational sex with a number of women, trying desperately to believe that he could be happy without commitment. Although he attended church in his childhood, he had no personal relationship with God. In his early twenties, while still in college, he surrendered his life to Christ. This truly transformed his life. However, in the recesses of his mind, the memories of his promiscuous past made him question if he could ever have a healthy relationship with a woman. He began dating Christian women in his local church, but he was constantly asking himself what would happen if they found out about his past. As the dating continued, his fears increased and he began questioning God. Why had God not intervened in those times of abuse and sexual acting out? He concluded that he was permanently damaged, something of a freak or misfit. He believed that in order to have God's blessing, he would need to become perfect. Only then would God bring a good woman into his life, a woman whom he could trust. If he could just be spiritually perfect, he would find the right mate and the new relationship would magically erase his whole past. Then he would be a perfect husband and prove his self-worth.

God did bring into his life a woman like no other before. She was caring, compassionate, loving, and godly. They married after only a brief dating relationship and started a family. She knew nothing about his past. He spoke little about his past, and then he told half-truths concerning his upbringing. As he observed his wife's godly words and actions, his sense of guilt increased. His wife's faith was real. She had the kind of transparency in her actions, thoughts, and behavior that he only dreamed about. His past began to haunt him as his wife grew spiritually and tried to establish a deeper relationship with him. He began to lie more about his past. In fact, he told her on more than one occasion that he had relationships with only a few women before her. Although he believed he could trust her with the truth, inwardly he feared that if she knew the truth their marriage would end. His old pattern of trusting no one, not even God, began to resurface.

His thoughts became anxious and obsessive: How could she love him? How would this godly woman react if she discovered the truth about his past? He worried that his wife would learn the truth and be disgusted with him. This worry began to dominate his life. His negative attitudes and anxieties controlled him, yet he felt he could not share the truth with her. As their marriage progressed, communication began to break down, resentment and frustration arose, and his fears of abandonment drove him to withdraw from his wife. Their sexual contacts became infrequent and she began asking what was wrong. Guilt about the past interfered with any intimacy he might have with his wife. He began to experience the same hopelessness about the past that he felt before their marriage, believing that no one, not even God, could help him now. He believed his wife deserved a better partner, and he would always be damaged beyond repair.

In healthy marital relationships, we know that we can trust our spouses with our emotional, physical, and spiritual well-being. Our trust is predicated on the confidence that our spouses have our best interests at heart, based upon the sacrificial love that Christ gives them for us. Doesn't this suggest how Christian couples can deal with unresolved issues of the past?

Our unresolved guilt can be dispelled by directly relying on God's promises of ultimate forgiveness. He offers to change and correct all of our past mistakes. First John 1:9 states that God forgives us of all things in the past and no longer holds anything to our account. God himself can cleanse us and bring forgiveness for our past sins if we will surrender our past to him. First Peter 5:7 promises that if we will cast our cares upon him, he will cleanse us from all the past.

> **In healthy marital relationships, we know that we can trust our spouses with our emotional, physical, and spiritual well-being.**

Do I tell my spouse...?

Of course, this leads to another question: When God forgives me and I accept his forgiveness, how open should I be in telling my spouse about what has been forgiven? I strongly recommend that you discuss this question with a Christian psychologist, counselor, or pastor before you make a decision of this magnitude. Ask your counselor whether telling your spouse about the past will be helpful in your present relationship. Ask whether such a revelation might damage your marriage when you intend to bring peace. This is not an attempt to hide anything from your spouse; it is simply making a candid assessment of your past so that you can gauge whether sharing it would have a direct, positive effect on the future of your marriage.

It is important to realize whether past sexual abuse or sexual misconduct is having a negative impact at this juncture in your marriage. If you bring these issues to the Lord and accept his forgiveness in the privacy of prayer, there may be no benefit or need to bring the same issues to your spouse. When you are able to forgive yourself through God's love, this may free you from the past. It may silence those old tapes of guilt and shame. New hope and a new life can be established. On the other hand, denial and repression of the past will only bring pain and keep you chained emotionally. Acceptance of God's love and forgiveness not only frees you from past mistakes but clears your past account, never to be placed on you again. God says that he forgives you and will never remember your indiscretions, ever. That in itself is freeing—so freeing that you may be able to establish a new relationship with the past erased. This is the first step in making your life and your marriage anew. Christ can free you from the past, restoring trust in the present.

Without trust, a marriage cannot survive, yet many couples neglect this engine mount when constructing their marriage. By allowing God to work in your thoughts and actions, you will begin to experience forgiveness like never before. Forgiveness will free you from the past. By praying for a new direction, individually and together, you will begin to see each other in a different light and be able to establish genuine trust in your relationship. If you have been unfaithful or otherwise hurtful to your spouse, you need to ask your spouse for forgiveness. You need to accept responsibility for your actions and humble yourself before God. He can give you both a new vision for your marriage. He can produce new actions and thought patterns within you, turning you away from old characteristics of the past. This whole process takes time, but Romans 12:1–2 promises that God can transform and renew the old you so that you become trustworthy.

Security and Respect

I would like to discuss the next two stabilizers together because they are truly interdependent. Security may be defined as making one safe from danger or hurt. Respect is showing honor or receiving admiration, leading to a sense of worth. At this point, ask yourself the following questions:

1. Do I feel safe and secure with my mate?
2. Do I show honor to and admiration for my spouse?
3. When I speak in a respectful manner to my spouse, do I feel disrespected in return?
4. Do I feel my spouse honors and admires me and what I believe in?

Most couples report that feeling secure in a relationship allows them to engage in open communication about their desires and needs, even during courtship. The more secure they feel as a couple, the more open they are in sharing their thoughts and feelings. Security is built on more than just actions; it requires a complete openness about yourself. It requires taking the time to understand the heart and soul of your partner. If you have never felt safe enough to share your emotions with your spouse, you are already experiencing great emotional loneliness in your marriage, a disconnection from the one you love. It can lead to separation.

I stated earlier that loss of trust may originate with family or childhood issues. The same is true with a person's feelings of insecurity. If you did not feel secure while growing up, it may be very difficult for you to feel secure with your spouse. Even when you have every outward reason to feel safe in your present relationship, something seems to hold you back. This can exacerbate feelings of depression, anxiety, and panic, causing you to retreat from your spouse emotionally.

One woman described the experience like this: "At first, I felt so safe in his arms. It was like the world stopped and I was at peace. As our marriage moved ahead, it started to change. He became so closed with everything, and those times of sharing just seemed to stop. I started feeling so alone. Everything seemed dark, and my anxiety increased to the point that I never felt safe in anything I was trying to do."

Establishing security

Security in marriage is created in several ways, and it can be revealed in several ways. For example, security can be created by:

- Words spoken
- Actions taken
- Consistency in words and actions each day

Review the following questions concerning security in your marriage:

1. Are you as gentle and caring with the words you use now with your spouse as you were when you were dating or at the beginning of your marriage?

2. Do you take time to listen to what your spouse is saying, or do you block out most of what is said?

These questions are for both genders, husbands and wives. Let's take a moment to apply them specifically:

Fellows, you can't hear your wife if you are already trying to formulate your response to her. You can't hear her if you do not focus your full attention on the words she says. (Turn off the TV, put down the newspaper, and so on.) Women often report in counseling that they feel a calm sense of reassurance if their spouses actively listen to them and allow them to share their thoughts and feelings openly.

Ladies, you can't hear your husband if you try to out-talk him when he is conversing with you. If what is taking place in his world clearly bores you, he will stop telling you about it. He will retreat to silence or other outside activities, which only creates more frustrations between the two of you.

Sharing feelings is often difficult for married couples, especially males. To communicate feelings openly together, you need to be patient. Take some quiet time together, just the two of you, to talk about things that deeply matter to each of you. This will establish safety in your communication. Choose words that allow you to share comfortably the thoughts and ideas about who you are and the direction you desire in this marriage. All of this requires openness. Be careful not to have a critical attitude when you begin this process. The closeness and openness you had during courtship may now be lost, due to critical comments you may have made or insecurities your spouse may have developed.

During courtship, you probably took time to explore and understand this unique and wonderful person God placed in your life. It was important to you both to know and understand each other deeply. Sharing together was fun and enjoyable because you were just getting to know each other. Listening was a priority. Are you still exploring new ways to enjoy being with your spouse? Has lack of time or lack of patience robbed you of this joy? It is time to reclaim it. Both of you may need to unlock emotional doors that you have been hiding behind and that have prevented you from sharing. You may fear what could happen if you open up to your spouse and she does not reciprocate. You may say, "I don't want to be vulnerable again and end up getting hurt." However, that is a risk worth taking.

If you rely on God to guide your communication, you can count on a positive outcome.

If you rely on God to guide your communication, you can count on a positive outcome. Start by sharing your fears, specifically fears of hurt and rejection. God is able to change your feelings and remove your fears, so it is important that you begin to pray for each other in this matter. Seek God's wisdom to help you feel safe in your marriage. You will find genuine security in your relationship if you strive for it together. Share your intimate thoughts and feelings; discuss the needs and desires that you both have. In many ways, it is a threefold endeavor:

- Be careful about your response to what your spouse says. Words spoken are like leaves blown from a tree: once they are gone, they cannot be retrieved.

- Talk openly about your innermost thoughts and desires for yourself and your marriage.

- Talk honestly about who you are and the expectations you have for your marriage, based upon what God has revealed to you.

If necessary, talk about problems from your past together, but do not feel obligated to do this. When talking with your spouse, you are not trying to be a historian of the relationship; this will only rob you of what you are trying to renew. You are now focusing on the future, not the past. Learn to be bright and colorful again in your actions and words. Learn to respond playfully to your mate. The Song of Solomon has some very colorful passages portraying Solomon's bride, who had stolen his heart. He describes her beauty and tells her how important she is to him. In the same passages, the woman expresses how important this man is to her and the closeness that she desires with him. Sharing together will open up profound expressions of love, just as it did for Solomon. Trust me, the two of you can have a deeper love again, and this expressive love will spark a new intimacy between you.

Intimacy involves a deep probing into your loved one's emotions, character, and innermost thoughts. Take time to rediscover your spouse's beauty. The more intimate you become with your mate, the more exciting and secure the relationship will be. Emotional intimacy allows your partner to know what you desire in your marriage.

Again, as a man, you may find it very difficult to talk about the feelings in your relationship. Some men see this as a sign of weakness or frailty, and some women find it difficult to share there feelings as well. However, as we've already discussed, we want to act toward our mates as Christ would. Christ showed his emotions appropriately and openly. In John 11:35, the words "Jesus wept" reveal the emotional transparency of Jesus. At his friend Lazarus's tomb, he experienced deep pain and openly expressed his sorrow for Lazarus's death. Men, take special note of this: *Christ showed his inward emotional pain outwardly to others.* Your wife wants to have a strong husband but not someone who is a stone wall when he is hurting emotionally. Women need to see your courage and strength, but they also want their husbands to share their vulnerability. They want their men to lean on them as well when problems arise. Depending on each other demonstrates the strength of your marriage, not weakness. Sharing your emotions is a sign that you have built genuine security in your relationship with each other and God. It enables you both to experience true closeness to one another when the storms of life arise. If you both will take the time to develop a secure relationship, then you will naturally express respect for one another.

Building respect

Remember, respect means having high regard or honor for someone else, holding someone in high esteem. This truly represents the essence of a committed relationship and points directly to the biblical principle of sacrificing oneself for the purpose of upholding and honoring the other person. Extreme damage is done to a marriage when mutual respect is lost. When you are unable to honor or hold your spouse in high esteem, your marriage is dying. This may happen suddenly, as with sexual infidelity, but too often respect is eroded by years of sarcasm, verbal attacks, and hurtful behavior excused with the phrase "I was just joking."

Once, while attending a dinner party with my wife, I was standing near a group of couples and overheard them talking. One of the men began to joke about his wife's weight. I was aware that she had always struggled with her weight, battling poor self-image and low self-esteem. It was evident by her experession that she was uncomfortable. Her husband, although a nice fellow, did not know when to put a lid on his comments. With one statement, he emotionally destroyed his wife in front of their friends. They were planning a cruise later that month, so the conversation went something like this:

"So, Bob, are you looking forward to that cruise?"

"Oh, you bet. I can't wait, there are so many places to stop and see. Mary and I will have the time of our lives."

"What exactly are you going to be seeing?"

"Well, there are several ports of call, and I hope we can explore as many things along the way as possible. I just hope I can keep Mary away from the buffet tables. With all that food around, she will be like a kid in a candy store. She never knows when to quit."

At this moment, everyone fell silent. Mary looked like she could cry. The rest of us felt very awkward, realizing the pain caused by what Bob had said. The problem was, Bob did not realize it and he kept on.

"You know, we both love to eat, but this is a real struggle for Mary. I will just have to push her through the line so she does not stop and graze." At this point, Bob started to laugh and shot a glance toward Mary. Seeing the downcast expression on her face, he finally got it. Then Bob uttered those famous works: "Honey, you know I'm just kidding."

Mary walked away in heartbroken silence. Bob understood exactly what he had done, but it was too late. His words were out—in public.

If you really want to destroy your spouse emotionally, just try joking and being sarcastic about her in public. (Ladies, this is an area of concern for you as well. Stop and think if there have been times when you have shown disrespect for your husband in front of others. I have been involved in several public conversations where a wife has torpedoed her husband about issues that should have been kept private, such as the man's inability to keep a job, pay bills, maintain the house, or satisfy her sexually.)

A husband and wife may lose respect for one another over a long period of time, after years of not speaking out or changing patterns of poor behavior. It is also possible to suddenly stop showing respect for each other; I see this when couples just stop caring about what is taking place with their marriage. I have counseled couples who say they respect each other but repeatedly humiliate their spouses in public. Why would someone do this to the person they say they love? Let's explore this for a moment. When one or both partners stop caring about the marriage, trust and security are no longer valued. Nothing is sacred in the marriage. Attacks on each other's character begin. At first, they may be comical in nature, but then the attacks become more open and destructive, until there is a total breakdown of the relationship.

As I have shared earlier, in order to renew your marriage, you must concentrate first on changing your own life. To build respect, each of you must consider what is required in your own lives for that change to take place. Determine what is required of you in order to stop the erosion of respect in your relationship. I use the word *required* because God commands you to honor the individual he has given you as a mate (see Eph 5:22—6:9; Col 3:18–4:1; 1 Pet 3:1–7). I know that at times you may feel as if you have been hurt beyond any possibility of repairing the marriage. Even when there has been a pattern of disrespectful behavior and broken promises, God can bring restoration to your marriage. First Corinthians 10:13 promises us that, no matter how difficult our situation, God provides a way for us to endure and find victory.

Forgetting the past

Again, the process starts with your asking God to change you—not only your heart, but also your mind. Seek your wife's forgiveness for the way you have responded to her, and ask her to work with you in building new levels of openness to reinvigorate your marriage relationship. God can remold the stabilizing values of trust, security and respect. For that to happen, you need to leave the past in God's hands and ask him to make a new future for you. By letting go of the past and no longer playing the old tapes of

> **You need to leave the past in God's hands and ask him to make a new future for you.**

customary behavior in your life, you and your spouse make a new commitment to each other before God. Ask him to allow you to be a servant to your spouse, to be sacrificial in your love, and to renew honor and respect in all areas of your marriage. Focus on moving ahead and putting the past behind you.

Complete the Diagnostic Evaluation on the next page before continuing.

DIAGNOSTIC EVALUATION

1. Am I willing to pray and ask God to renew my heart and mind to his image, changing old patterns and behaviors in order to love my spouse anew?

2. What memories of past conflict may cause me to hesitate before making these changes?

3. Is there any resentment or bitterness between us?

4. Am I ready to let go of the past and focus only on the present and future?

5. Am I willing to ask my spouse to forgive me for the harm I have caused, resulting in a loss of trust, security or respect?

5. CHECKING THE ALIGNMENT

5. CHECKING THE ALIGNMENT
UNDERSTANDING AND COMMUNICATING
NEEDS AND EXPECTATIONS

"I can do all things through Christ, who strengthens me."
—*Philippians 4:13* NKJV

Kim and Mike became acquainted while in college. They enjoyed having fun together. It was a lot more fun to go to parties with a familiar friend instead of going by themselves or trying to ask for a date. In fact, their relationship revolved around parties and alcohol. Their friends just assumed that they were a couple because they were together so often. Before long, the title *couple* seemed to fit them because they always had a good time together. They enjoyed each other's company and weekends went well. It wasn't long before they started having sexual relations. Their sex encounters were more recreational than intimate, because most of the time they had been drinking.

Kim had been a Christian but had abandoned her relationship with God when she entered college. Life was completely different away from home and her family, church, and old friends. Even so, she always believed that someday she would return to her spiritual roots and raise her children in the faithful and secure kind of home she had experienced. Mike was raised by his single mother and rarely saw his father. They had been divorced when he was three. He had never known a personal relationship with God. Mike thought college was where he would find himself. He wanted a good degree and a great job in order to have all the things he had been denied because of his mom's situation. Mike and Kim never discussed this disparity in their backgrounds and aspirations; they just enjoyed the fun they had in the present.

Kim didn't think she really loved Mike, though he was a nice guy and treated her well. She admired Mike for being an excellent student who planned to get a high-quality job after graduation. (This wasn't a quality she found in a lot of the guys she had met in college.) He could make her laugh, and he liked to talk. Once in a while, they even discussed spiritual matters, but this sometimes led to arguments, so Kim avoided talking about her beliefs.

For his part, Mike liked spending time with Kim. She was physically attractive, and the sex was really good. She made Mike feel good about himself, and he didn't have to worry about her getting too serious. She seemed to just enjoy their time together, as he did. Kim wasn't someone he planned to marry, but he occasionally thought that might change.

Change it did. One weekend, after drinking too much and having sex that neither of them could remember, their lives changed forever. The month ended with Kim missing her period. Before long, it was obvious that Kim was pregnant. Mike's first solution was to pay for Kim to have an abortion. He was surprised when she refused. She had seemed so level-headed until now, but she started saying that she knew God didn't want her to kill their baby. She really seemed resolute in this. He didn't feel he could let her go through the pregnancy alone.

As they discussed the situation, Mike thought that maybe they should get married. He was almost done with school and Kim only had a year to go. They both thought marriage was the answer to their baby problem. Mike would get a decent job and somehow everything would be all right. Kim had some reservations because she didn't know if she really loved Mike, and she always had planned on marrying a Christian. But she was determined to make this marriage work because of the baby. She started telling herself that maybe she really did love Mike. After all, they had fun together.

Maybe they didn't share their deepest thoughts and desires, but that could come later.

Soon after their wedding, the problems began. Mike did get a job, though it wasn't what he had hoped for. They felt an out-of-state move was impossible due to the baby. Kim had a very hard pregnancy and delivery. Caring for a baby was more work than she ever imagined. It seemed to suck the energy right out of her. The baby didn't bring the joy and contentment Kim had expected, either. Having a child just widened the distance between Mike and her. Mike felt no responsibility to care for the baby, after all, Kim had insisted on having it. Now she seemed tired and grouchy most of the time. She didn't give him any attention. He was lucky if she even fixed dinner once in a while. Sex was rare and seemed to just be something that Kim wanted to be over as quickly as possible. At this juncture, Mike started staying out late with friends and renewed his partying habits from college. Kim was miserable at home. Before long, she ended up in my office.

"Dr. Vaughn, I just don't know what to do," she said. "What have I done? I don't even know this man, and he definitely doesn't know me!"

Tears flowed down Kim's cheeks as she continued. "All my hopes and dreams are gone! This isn't what I thought my marriage would be. What do I do now?" At twenty-four years of age, Kim felt her life had become a prison sentence. Depressed, anxious, and overwhelmed, she just wanted to make it all go away.

As you read this story, you may see little connection to your situation. Your relationship may

As men, our needs are often unspoken, but ultimately we hope that we have found a woman who will fulfill them.

have been nothing like this in the beginning. But a shaky beginning in a couple's relationship often prompts a number of why questions later in the marriage. We come to marriage with certain needs and expectations that we hope will be met by our partner. These needs include what we want for ourselves, the other person, and the relationship itself. As men, our needs are often unspoken, but ultimately we hope that we have found a woman who will fulfill them. Even when needs aren't met in the beginning of the relationship, a man may tell himself that as he bonds with his woman, she will understand him better and will therefore be able to meet his needs.

Sometimes, out of a fear of abandonment or loss, a man will deceive himself into believing his needs are being met when they aren't. In his quest to find a mate, he may also project an image of someone he is not. In that case, he hopes that he will be able to adapt to what his girlfriend expects in order to be loved and respected. In essence, he denies his own personality, creating a façade which he can't maintain later in the relationship.

I deal with couples who have been married a significant number of years, and they often state that at the beginning of their relationship each partner had tried to transform themselves into what the other person expected. Many have continued to strive to keep the façade in place. But as the marriage progresses, at least one partner becomes unable or unwilling to maintain the status quo. I hear statements such as, "She was so different when we were dating!" "He used to know what I was thinking." "She doesn't even try to show any respect for me." "He isn't the same person. I don't love him now."

Assessing your relationship

This painful realization can begin a time of crisis or a time of transformation. Consider the following questions:

- Were you open and real with your wife in your dating?

- Did you try to meet the expectations of your mate to an extent that you knew deep down you weren't capable of maintaining?

- Did you in fact know your wife's needs and expectations for her future? Do you think her expectations are being met now?

- Are your expectations for your marriage being met?

- Have you become disconnected from your wife on any level, or on a number of levels?

Couples move through several predictable stages during courtship. A review of these stages will allow you to assess the history of your relationship.

Acquaintance stage
"So do you live around here?"
Fellows, this is the stage when you were unsure whether your partner would even want to know who you were. Some men are good at generating the superficial talk that allows communication, but no depth, at this stage. Perhaps you were one of them. You could talk about the weather, school, jobs, without any real fear of getting hurt or rejected. This was the safe zone of your relationship—nothing ventured, nothing lost. However, this stage only lasts a short time. A decision is made by both of you about whether you will proceed to a possible relationship.

Friendship stage
"Maybe we could hang out sometime"
Here's where courtship often gets a little tricky. If the woman says, "No, thanks," engine shutdown occurs and you have to do some backtracking. Nobody wants to be rejected, but at this stage you open yourself up for possible rejection. If the woman says, "Yes," your engine begins running and shifts into gear. You take time to listen to her. You find out who she is, what she likes,

what she dreams for the future. Wives tell me that a meaningful connection was being made at this stage, so they wanted to know you better. Why? You looked at her. You listened to her. You engaged her at all levels: physically, emotionally, and perhaps even spiritually.

Intimate friendship stage

"I want to know everything about you"

When we invite another person into the deepest parts of our lives, we become vulnerable. Opening up to a woman and letting yourself become transparent to her creates a deep connection that allows her to understand the real you. You learn about each other's hobbies and experiences. You find out what makes her happy and what makes her sad. You tell her things that you've never shared with anyone before. You learn the people and experiences of her life that molded her into the woman before you. You learn to make each other laugh. Think of your own wife right now. What is her favorite ice cream? What type of food might she want to get late at night just for the fun of it? Remember sitting in her driveway sharing your past, your fears, and your dreams? Remember how you didn't want her to have to go inside? Remember calling her as soon as you got home (in the era before cell phones)? Remember laughing together over something so simple that no one else could understand it? All of these experiences start the bonding process. This sharing creates trust, and this trust must remain sacred in marriage. This bonding leads you to become best friends and ultimately "one." This bonding is a lifetime endeavor, but it can be betrayed with a thoughtless comment at a party, such as, "That's nothing! My wife is so uptight she wet the bed until the ninth grade!" or "She's always afraid people will think she is out of place."

It is easy to take for granted the trust we have built over a lifetime. It's easy to forget to take the time to share yourself with your wife. She still likes to hear about your struggles, your fears, and your dreams. You wake up with her. You eat with her. You sleep with her. Do you share your feelings with her? Do you laugh with her? Do you ask about her?

Perhaps you feel you did not truly get to know your wife before marriage. That takes time and extensive sharing. Many couples skip this crucial stage of their relationship and engage in sexual intimacy after a few dates. Their relationship is then more of a sexual nature than a personal one. Others develop a superficial friendship in which they were buddies with their partners. Then, like Mike and Kim, they allow circumstances to carry them along with little thought.

Needs and expectations

Now, you may not have been a couple who became sexually intimate in the early stages of your relationship, but it is still possible that you missed developing a deep understanding of "knowing" the other person. When this happens, a couple fails to identify one another's needs and expectations. Ask yourself, did you allow your relationship just to happen? If so, it is time to shift into gear and become intentional about developing your relationship with your wife.

In counseling, I often ask couples to do a homework assignment of listing their needs in four specific areas:

- Physical needs
- Emotional needs
- Social needs
- Spiritual needs

One definition of *need* is "not having enough of the things essential for an adequate standard of living." These four areas of need must be fulfilled sufficiently for you, as a couple, to have an adequate marriage relationship.

Expectations are different. We may suppose that our expectations are necessary requirements as well, but they often far exceed our real needs. Let me illustrate.

Joe worked within walking distance of his apartment until he became a victim of downsizing and had to look for a new job. He accepted a position that was better than his old job, but he now needed a car in order to get to work. There was no mass-transit system in his small town, and he had no money for a car. Hearing of his dilemma, a good friend offered him the use of his old car. It wasn't much to look at, but it was reliable. Joe thanked his friend but turned down the offer. He believed that he really needed a new car to make a good impression with his new employer.

Joe had a need—a car. Joe also had an expectation—a new car. Now don't get me wrong; I'm not trying to compare marital needs to an old car. But do you see that we often confuse what we need with what we expect? Joe may not be able to afford a new car now, but any car will do for the moment. Let's say that Joe works at his new job, saves his money, and then is able to buy his new car. He has then met both a need and an expectation. However, fulfilling the need comes first.

Men often confuse expectations with needs. You probably shared many of your needs with your wife during your courtship. At the same time, you had expectations of how she could meet those needs in ideal ways, and you may not have shared those. Everything seemed wonderful. She was your soul mate. She understood you. She got you. However, she really didn't have a clue of your expectations. She knew some of your needs. She may have tried to meet your needs through her own expectations of the relationship. But you may feel cheated because you really thought she understood your expectations, and she didn't. This lack of communication is the root of discontent in many marriages.

As mentioned earlier, I will have couples start working on this problem by having each partner make a needs list. It must include needs from each of the four categories. Each person will discuss this list with me individually and then together as a couple. I ask them to look specifically at each other's priorities in these areas. Are they surprised at their spouse's list? To what degree can they meet these needs in the marital relationship? How are they being met now? As we review the separate lists of the husband and wife, I ask them to look carefully for any expectations in either list. (I will ask you and your wife to complete this exercise at the end of this chapter.) The focus is directed toward meeting the needs each person has. This is a difficult exercise for most couples and must be done prayerfully.

When needs go unmet

When an individual's needs are not met, a sequence of destructive events takes place. You may have already experienced some of these events in your marriage. When your needs are not being met, you experience emotional hurt. Early in your relationship, you felt you could trust your wife to fulfill the needs you expected to be fulfilled in your marriage. If they were, you felt secure. If your needs were not met, your respect for her began to dwindle. That wasn't how it was supposed to be. This produces a feeling of rejection, which grows if nothing changes within your relationship. Resentment follows. You may even begin to question your wife's love for you. You wonder, Why doesn't she love me enough to meet my needs? Is something wrong with me? Why is she so insensitive? She cares about everybody but me! What happened to the wonderful woman I trusted to be my soul mate?

If nothing happens to relieve your pain, you eventually begin to feel angry. You can deny your emotional pain for only so long. If you repress your anger, feelings of self-doubt, anxiety, and physical symptoms may occur. You may start having conflicts at work or in your other relationships. You may develop headaches, stomach problems, and more. If you express your anger outwardly, it can manifest as bitterness, resentment, or passive-aggressive behavior. If you find no resolution to your unmet needs at this point in the cycle, guilt and shame may follow. You feel embarrassed by your volatile, destructive behavior toward your wife and others.

Communication is the key. Since communication is often severely impaired in these situations, the cycle is hard to break without professional help. The following diagram illustrates what happens when you do not meet each other's needs.

DIAGRAM A

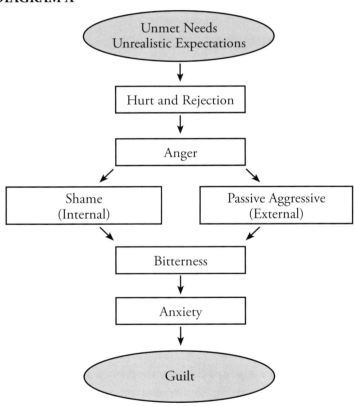

If you don't work to resolve these issues, the vicious cycle leaves you with little energy. You or your wife may begin to feel there isn't anything left to fight for. Finally, a break occurs. One or both of you will withdraw emotionally and physically from the other. This stage is usually characterized by the cycle in Diagram B.

DIAGRAM B

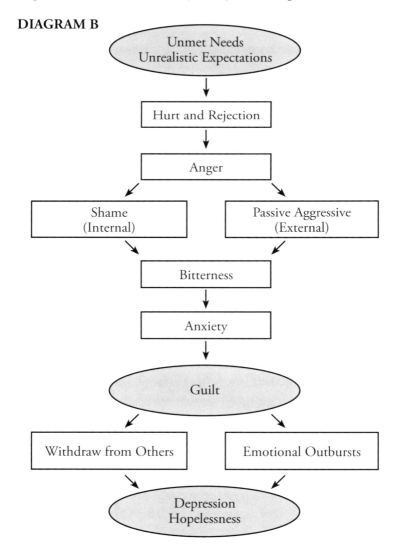

Remember, this situation is set in motion by unmet needs and faulty expectations in your marriage. At this juncture, many couples begin to think that divorce is the only solution. In the last stages of hopelessness and despair, they begin to feel numb. They perceive that they have a loveless, lifeless marriage.

Breaking out of the cycle

Is there any way to stop this downward spiral? Yes, there is. It begins by focusing on God's promises of freedom and hope for the most troubled marriage. For example, we read in Ecclesiastes: "Enjoy life with the woman whom you love all the days of your fleeting life which he has given you under the sun" (9:9 NASB). This is God's plan. Your marriage can be satisfying and full of love, specifically later in life. If you feel trapped in a cycle of unfulfilled needs and unrealized expectations, don't take the detour of divorce. Claim God's promises for you and your spouse.

I often hear troubled couples say, "It's not that bad, but I don't have the tools to fix it." If you feel that way, read the following questions carefully. They are intense and challenging. Try to answer each one truthfully for yourself, and then ask your wife to do the same. It is very important to be open with your wife and ask her to do the same for you.

- Have there been times in the past in which you felt more emotional and physical contentment in your marriage than you do right now?

- How long has it been since you have felt a true desire to be with your wife?

- Did you feel a true closeness in your courtship and/or the early days of your marriage?

- Can you honestly say that you truly understand your wife's needs at the present time?

- Are you talking openly with your wife? Are you listening and trying to understand how to better to meet her needs?

- Have you withdrawn from your spouse because of persistent depression or sadness?

No couple has said, "I do," just to begin a tolerable marriage. If your marriage is just "tolerable" or becoming intolerable, identify where you are in the cycle (see Diagram B). Too often a couple comes to my office with raw emotions because one or both partners have withdrawn from the relationship. They may have chosen to let the marriage limp along for years, as it seems easier not to deal with their problems. It takes a great deal of energy to recover trust, respect, and intimacy at this point, but the cycle can be broken. You can work together to build a closer bond than you've ever had before. Take control of your marriage and determine to change it. Make a firm commitment to develop a better marriage than you've had. Open, honest communication is the key to dealing with the issues that have brought you to this point.

Discuss with your wife what positive changes should be made within your marriage. Even if you've not had good listening skills to this point, you can become a better listener as she shares her thoughts and feelings with you. Here are some tips:

- Ask for clarification when you don't understand what she is telling you.

- Listen to what she says she needs you to provide, without worrying about your own needs while she is talking.

- Summarize what you have heard her say and ask for clarification if you're not "getting it."

It is imperative to focus on what you have contributed to the problems in your marriage and what you can do to make a positive change. Discuss openly what you feel you can give your wife. Clearly identify what your wife is asking of you. Have a servant's heart so that the pain and hurt of the past can be replaced with God's love in you. It is often harder for men to share their own needs, but give her your trust. Share your needs with her. Don't revert back to faultfinding and complaining. Be honest about your needs and expectations for the marriage. Your brokenness can be healed as you turn in this more positive direction.

Here is another promise that God gives for dealing with any perplexing situation, including a troubled marriage: "Call to me and I will answer you and tell you great and unsearchable things you do not know" (Jer 33:3). There is hope for your marriage. If you and your wife are willing to be guided by the Lord, your marriage can be saved.

"But you do not understand how depressed and overwhelmed I am," you may say. "You don't know how disconnected we are!" It may feel as if the marriage is dead, but you can change the very foundation of your marriage if you reconnect to God's promises, ask for your mate's forgiveness, and seek God's wisdom for the future. Positive results will follow, though it does take time.

 **Complete the Diagnostic Evaluation on the next page before continuing.**

DIAGNOSTIC EVALUATION

The following evaluation should be done as a couple.

1. Place these headings at the top of a piece of paper: *physical needs, emotional needs, social needs,* and *spiritual needs.* Under each heading, list five things that you believe are the needs you seek to fulfill in your marriage. Ask your wife to do the same.

2. Review your lists separately for a few days, praying that God will reveal specifically if these are appropriate needs and not just expectations. Next, look over each other's list. Prayerfully consider needs versus expectations. Point out any items that your spouse has listed which you believe are expectations instead of needs. Listen to why your spouse thinks these items are needs. Try to come to an understanding of each other's needs.

3. Find a quiet place to talk together. Actively listen to what hurt and pain you have caused your wife. Acknowledge these hurts and ask your wife's forgiveness. Talk openly about what steps you need to take in order to restore trust and security. Remember, this is not a time to reopen old wounds from the past. Ask God to give you a new perspective on your marriage.

4. Recognize and accept your responsibility for your spouse's unmet needs. Take charge in meeting those needs from now on. Begin to speak openly with one another about your personal needs, without pressuring one another to perform.

5. Ask God to remove any bitterness or resentment you have harbored in your own heart against your spouse.

6. Take time to pray together, asking God to renew a new spirit in your heart and create a servant's heart toward your spouse. Claim the promise of Philippians 4:13, which says, "I can do all things through Christ, who strengthens me" (NKJV).

6. RECHARGING THE BATTERY

6. RECHARGING THE BATTERY
PUTTING THE SPARK BACK INTO ROMANCE

"I am my lover's and my lover is mine." —Song of Solomon 6:3

You should be in a passionate love affair with your spouse. Passion is a strong affection involving the deep love of someone or something. The passion between you and your wife should be strong and closely intertwined. Passion is essential to romance.

Romance is fun

All married people desire romance, especially wives. This is not to say that men do not care about romance, but some men seem to place a lower priority on it after a few years of marriage. It is possible that romance was never present, even during courtship, but the absence of romance will hinder the development of your marriage. Romance literally means having fun together. It means taking time to play together. You may recall memorable times in your relationship when you and your wife played in the snow, went sledding, had snowball fights, walked together in a park, tossed a football, or wrestled in a pile of autumn leaves. That kind of playfulness will keep romance alive in your relationship. Married couples enjoy the romance of walking together under a full moon or sitting by a fire while it crackles and pops as you snuggle under a blanket together. A romantic interlude doesn't require a great deal of money, but it does involve being creative and allowing the kid in you to emerge. Of course, romance can include different activities for men and women.

One man told me what attracted him to his wife as they were dating. As he put it, "She was not a super athlete, but she had spunk. She would run through the leaves, throw a football, or just laugh and joke with me. We were in our twenties, but we had so much childlike fun together! After we married, things changed. She doesn't seem to have time for those childlike things that attracted me to her in the beginning. I miss those times. For me, they were what made our relationship so special."

Women may be surprised to learn that men want playmates. Even in later years, guys want to play. Unfortunately, if they can't play with their wives, they will be tempted to play with someone else. Fun times are often reminiscent of your courtship. Your openness to one another during these relaxing, fun activities can refresh the communication between you.

Of course, this is not to say that only men want fun and adventure. Most women do too. One described her husband like this: "He used to go bike riding with me and enjoyed it. Now he says that it takes too long and he is tired. He sits and watches TV. I enjoyed those bike rides because they gave us time to talk together. I got a chance get to know him away from our work, away from the children, and away from the hustle and bustle of our lives. That playfulness actually allowed physical intimacy to develop between us, but now it seems to have disappeared." From her perspective (and that of many women), the following formula holds true throughout life:

Romance + Intimacy = Love

Ask yourself, when was the last time the two of you snuggled up together without having it end in sex? In all my counseling sessions, I have not found one woman who did not desire those special times of being with her husband, having his arms around her, embracing and feeling close to him—without feeling the pressure to perform sexually.

(You may say that you like physical closeness as well, you just wish there was a sexual part. Is there anything wrong with that? The answer, of course, is no. However, to rebuild a love affair, you need times to cherish each other without it always leading to sex. Sexual behavior is very important for every marriage, but meaningful sexual intimacy must be based on a true emotional connection. Unless there is a true emotional connection between you, the sexual component of your relationship will be poor. In fact, the sexual component may be missing altogether.)

Appearance and physical attraction

This section deals with some sensitive issues that may create emotional pain for both of you. I recommend that you and your spouse take time to read this individually before discussing it together. In order to build romance in your marriage, we need to discuss a number of relational aspects that can be very painful if they are missing or inadequate in your relationship. We will address these issues from both the male and female perspective. Just keep in mind that our purpose is to establish and enhance romance in your marriage by creating an environment conducive to emotional closeness and genuine unity.

Men are visually wired
Many women have a limited understanding of how their outward appearance affects a man's perception of them. Most women understand that men are visually stimulated, but they do not understand how basic images from the past can stay with a man for years, being played over and over at any given time. Men have a kind of radar that pulls them toward attractive images. An attractive woman can

pass in front of your husband and her image is immediately stored. Even for Christian men, these images can lead to other, more seductive images and thoughts that they do not wish to stay in their memory but cannot erase. The book *Every Man's Battle*, by Stephen Arterburn and others, discusses in detail how men should direct their eyes. It is such an important aspect of male psychology that husbands and wives both need to understand and discuss it. The images that a husband sees and the desires created in his mind can influence how he views his wife.

Ladies, I must say again that it is so important for you to understand this: *The images men see do not leave their minds for years and can later intrude in their thoughts.* Do not think that there is something evil about your husband when this happens. It is how men are made, so they must deal with it daily. God had a wholesome procreative plan for the visual connection he gave us as men. When sexual thoughts and images are left unchecked, unfortunately, they can destroy a marriage. They can lead men into behavior they would not otherwise contemplate.

When sexual thoughts and images are left unchecked, unfortunately, they can destroy a marriage.

In fact, ladies, let's look at an example of how men are visually wired. It is a hot summer day and you decide to go to the beach with your husband. You both feel that some sun and sand, mixed with beach recreational activities, would be fun and relaxing. Upon arriving, you find a nice place, put your chairs in the sand, spread your towels, slather the suntan lotion on, and you are ready to take it easy. You are sitting there talking and enjoying yourselves when suddenly "Ms. I Am Too Big For My Bikini" walks up and decides to put her chair beside you. You notice your husband wants to look at her, almost as if a magnet is pulling him. He can't seem to keep his head from turning to look at her. At this point, you become annoyed. Under your breath, you begin to ask yourself what his problem is.

Ok, ladies, here is the problem. Your husband is in the middle of a fire storm, with every aroused thought and visual neuron being connected and fired in his brain. Unfortunately, the more he tries not to look, the more the image intensifies. Men will sit in my office and describe these scenarios in great detail. It's not only women on the beach in bikinis; the same thing can happen with a secretary at work, a waitress in a restaurant, or just an attractive woman walking down the aisle in the grocery store. Men often tell me about this strong urge to stare at a female passing by. If he does stare and the stare remains unchecked, his desire can grow even further into a sexual longing.

Men, we must be well aware that we are wired to be attracted to beautiful things, but we have the ability to control our eyes as well. Remember, God's Word tells us that "we take captive every thought to make it obedient to Christ" (2 Cor 10:5). Unfortunately, seductive images that are stored in a man's thoughts become connected to new images within seconds, and this can lead to unwelcome desires.

In my senior year of high school, I worked nights in a grocery store. While stocking shelves, we guys were keenly aware of any young, attractive girl who entered the store. We had a code to alert one another when this happened. If an attractive female entered, we would stop our work and announce over the PA system that there was a "clean-up on Aisle 5." This was our signal to move toward that aisle. Many high school girls knew exactly what we were doing, but it was truly harmless and done in fun. In counseling sessions today, I hear some married men say that they still have this desire to follow an attractive woman in a store, moving from aisle to aisle just to get a glimpse of her. These are not perverted men who are prone to stalking. These are normal men—yes, even Christian men. They will ask me why they still do this, even though they are very happily married. Beauty and sexuality are magnets that know no age limit. The answer to changing this behavior involves taking control of every thought and action.

Remember, men, taking every thought captive is a continual task. It is important for a male to learn early in life how to control the images he focuses on and the desires he harbors in his heart. These will have lasting effects on his thought life for years to come. Very few women have a problem with the visual triggers that I am describing. Therefore, ladies, it may be difficult for you to comprehend the struggle that your husband can have with lustful thoughts and images that pass through his mind. As his wife, you can help him by being aware of situations where these temptations will cross his path. For example, in the beach scenario I described earlier, you could tell your husband that you feel uncomfortable and would like to move to a different spot. Your husband will likely agree with you and be grateful for the suggestion. (Men, although your first response may be to stay and "enjoy the view," *take every thought captive*.) Most husbands are not trying to be unfaithful in their thought life, but you can help each other if you are willing to be honest and communicate about these potential battles.

Men, let's candidly admit we are sexually driven beings, and these sex drives can be triggered by a myriad of images we encounter on a daily basis. I find it interesting to watch guys attend a professional football game. Between quarters, a team of attractive cheerleaders run onto the field—for what purpose? Now do not jump to the conclusion that I think cheerleading is wrong; it does excite spectators to become involved at a game. Even so, at a professional basketball or football game, most men do not look at the cheerleaders in order to be able to cheer louder! We look because of the alluring dress and movement of these women.

This may seem so simple that you may ask why I am even commenting on this. It illustrates how wives and husbands are different. At times, it is automatic for a man's thoughts to be preoccupied by the attractiveness of a woman sitting or standing in front of him. These images can stimulate sexual desires that are powerful. Husbands, at such times, you must be committed to refocus your mind in ways that bring honor to God, your wife and family. You can protect yourself from impure thoughts by being attentive to where you are and what you are viewing. It may be necessary to remove yourself from the immediate situation for a period of time, or longer, if the situation warrants it. You may even need to consider avoiding situations altogether that you know are stumbling blocks to pure thoughts.

Be proactive rather than reactive to the temptation. It is a good idea to have another Christian male as an accountability partner with whom you can meet on an consistent basis. Discuss your weaknesses with him and how you might protect yourself from temptations. You and your accountability partner should pray about your particular issues. God can place a hedge around you.

Wives, beauty catches men's attention, so you can be sure that beauty will catch your husband's attention. It is not unusual for your husband to notice when an attractive woman enters the room. However, that does not automatically mean he desires that woman over or more than you. Nor does it mean that his feelings have changed for you, his wife. If your relationship is emotionally solid, no other woman's beauty or attractiveness will change the relationship that the two of you have.

So my counsel to wives is this: Do not imagine unfaithfulness that does not exist. On the other hand, discuss openly the emotions you feel when he is in these situations. This will help him better understand what you are experiencing when these temptations present themselves. By speaking openly to each other now, you will establish communication patterns to help you deal with such distractions. It may sound simple, but you need to pray for wisdom and protection for each other as you proceed in these areas. The greatest gift that you can give your husband is to guard against unwanted temptations and stressors. Forethought is needed concerning outings and activities. Plan ahead so you can avoid

> **My counsel to wives is this: Do not imagine unfaithfulness that does not exist.**

events or situations that could be distracting or temptations for your husband. Of course, you cannot anticipate every possibility, but be proactive in your planning. If you find yourselves in a situation where a sexually arousing stimulus presents itself, be willing to talk about how you can leave or change the situation. You are not trying to be your husband's monitor. You are trying to be his advocate. Talk openly together regarding this issue.

Wives, your appearance matters

Now let's turn again to the subject of your own appearance and self-image. Hopefully, ladies, you now better understand how female beauty does impact your relationship with your husband. I hope that both of you see how men are "wired" differently in this respect, and their response to visual stimulus can impact your relationship. Your outward appearance—weight, clothing, hair, etc.—does matter to your husband. He may not want to tell you how he sees you, out of fear of hurting your feelings. However, your appearance is a major factor in how your husband responds to you both sexually and emotionally. It is not that he wants you to be a perfect ten. He wants to be pleased with how you look and proud that you are his wife. You may feel frustrated with the fact that I am focusing on the wife's appearance and weight because you know there is no way to look as you did when you were dating your husband. You have borne children, you are older, and you do not feel that you can compete with those women on television. Or you might be asking yourself why your husband can't just love you the way you are.

I want you to reflect on the following questions. Pay close attention. This is not a message to a wife that she must go back and somehow be thin and perfect in appearance again. We are all aware of how the media, especially television, can be exploitive of a woman's body image. The focus here may be better addressed by the following questions and comments that come up over and over again when men speak to me in counseling concerning their wife's appearance. Review these for insight and as a way of opening up some conversation between the two of you on a very touchy subject.

"Why has she let herself go?"
"Why doesn't she to care about her weight?"
"She used to look nice for me. Now it doesn't even seem to matter to her."

Wives, your husbands talk about whether good health is a priority to you. They speak very openly to me about the fact that they wish their wives would try to stay in shape, exercise regularly, and eat right. I seldom hear husbands asking for more when they are addressing this topic. They want their wives to be attractive and stay in shape. They want you to take care of the body that God has given you. You may wonder why this is so important to men at all. Remember that God caused your husbands to desire you and created men to seek beauty with their eyes. We look for outward beauty as well as inward beauty. Reflect on your courtship and you will probably remember times when you took extra care concerning your clothing, weight, and overall appearance. You likely strived to keep all of those factors in proper balance. If you have always had a poor self image or body image, achieving that balance may have been a problem that you dealt with and continue to deal with today. The difference is that you can now dialogue openly with your spouse about your physical health and appearance.

Ladies, read carefully this summary of a conversation that took place in a counseling session:

"Bill, the woman you are romantically involved with, describe her outward appearance," I said.

"I don't know, Doc," Bill replied. "She's kind of like my wife, but different."

"How different? Is she younger, thinner, prettier?"

"Maybe a little thinner. She just takes care of herself better, I guess. She always looks good for me, and her perfume smells great. Her eyes, her hair, her lips—everything just seems to glisten," Bill said.

"So do you mean she is more attractive than your wife, or is she just more appealing to you?"

Bill thought for a moment. "I see what you mean. She just makes herself more appealing. She is always fixed up, put together. Funny, now that you ask, she looks much like my wife did years ago. I never realized that, to be honest. She is not naturally more beautiful than my wife. She just fixes herself up for me."

Now, ladies, before you throw this book down and stop reading, please know that I am not condoning Bill's actions. But this conversation plays out often when I counsel with husbands who become unfaithful to their wives. They inevitably make two statements about the other woman: (1) "She fixes herself up for me." (2) "She makes me feel special."

Ladies, this is important. Men want their wives to take care of their appearance. They work with women who dress professionally every day. Whether you work inside or outside the home, the way you look when your husband walks in the door after work will speak volumes to him. Yes, your evenings are busy. It is important to realize, though, that your husband compares your appearance with what he has seen of other women all day. All of us want to get out of our work clothes when we come home, so you may be inclined to slip into an old jogging suit or jeans that do not quite fit you anymore. Such clothing sends a message of carelessness to your husband that you most likely do not intend to send. As visual beings, men's inward feelings are shaped by what they see outwardly, whether they realize it or not.

Focus on how you can both please each by talking openly about what is important and appropriate. It will take trust, commitment and sensitivity for both of you to be able to share concerning this critical area. The purpose of this conversation is not to be demeaning but to enhance the closeness of your relationship by sharing what physically pleases each of you about the other.

Husbands, your appearance matters

Every man has heard how important it is to communicate honestly with his wife. This certainly applies to finding out what your wife wants to see, smell, and feel when she comes into contact with you. Men, if you will take the time to truly understand your wife's needs, you will strengthen your marriage. So let us turn our attention to what men need to understand about what is attractive to females.

A man's physical appearance is a major factor in the way a woman views him. I often hear men joking together about being overweight. They make fun of how large their stomachs have become, as if they

A man's physical appearance is a major factor in the way a woman views him.

were public testimonies to their wives' good cooking. A man might say, "Hey, I am about eight months pregnant!" Then he shows his buddies how huge his belly is, as if it were something to be proud of. They laugh, but the man's wife finds this less amusing. Why? Because obesity is not what attracted her to him. I have heard many women say that they wish their husbands would lose some weight. When they were first married, their mates were fit and trim. Now their husbands wear excess weight proudly, as if it were a trophy. As one woman put it, "It disgusts me. It turns me off emotionally as well as sexually." Many women work in a professional environment with men who take pride and care in their appearance. She would not hear most of them making light of their lack of physical condition.

Guys, I am not arguing that your wife wants you to be Mr. Universe! She just wants you to strike a healthy balance in your life. How you take care of your own body reflects greatly on how you care for your wife. No wife wants to take care of an overweight, diabetic male who needs a knee replacement at age fifty-five.

I am not trying to paint a dismal picture of middle-aged couples. However, carelessness about our physical health is a real problem that erects real barriers between middle-aged spouses. These issues affect your wives' respect for you, husbands. This need not be a problem if you take time to stay in good physical shape and be aware that this affects not only your physical attractiveness but your ability to have sexual relations. Weight can and does have a tremendous impact both on the desire for lovemaking and on lovemaking itself. Take responsibility for your health in order to please your wife as well as yourself. She wants to be proud of you when you both go out in public. She wants you to look good. There are many physical activities you can do as a couple (e.g., walking, biking, hiking) that will help both of you to stay in shape. Such activities not only allow you to exercise but also to communicate with one another in the process.

Remember, guys, I am not challenging you to regain the physical appearance you had when you were twenty years old. However, you can show your wife that you really care for her by paying attention to your health. Just as it is very important for her to be in good physical shape, it is equally important for you to maintain your appearance and physical health.

Now, let's consider the husband's appearance at home. When a man arrives home from work, it is easy to throw on the same old flannel shirt and pair of old jeans that are too small, stained and paint-spattered, and should have been thrown away years ago. Many wives complain that their husbands look nice for everyone else all day, but the minute they come home, they revert to the same rerun every night. Well, men, here's a bulletin: your wife wants you to look handsome for her at home as well as in public.

Take extra care to look nice for her when you go out together. During the dating years, most men automatically try to smell good and look good by dressing attractively. Women still want that after you've been married for a few years. Here are some comments made by wives:

"I want people to see my husband and say, 'Wow, he looks nice!'"

"I feel like he cares more about me when he puts on nice clothes and cologne. It does not need to be anything fancy, just nice and clean."

"When he dresses up for me, it says he respects me, he cares about me, and he wants me to be proud of him."

During dating, men learn that little things about personal hygiene are important. After a few years of marriage, a husband often forgets this. He may start to view his wife as a kind of trophy that no longer needs to be treasured. The prize has been won. However, God's Word contains a very significant comment about this: "Husbands ought to love their wives as their own bodies" (Eph 5:28). Treating your wife in special ways is as important as your caring for your own body. Look into the mirror. Be willing to change and do what you must to make your wife proud of your appearance. Do not let stubbornness stand in your way.

Be the white knight

Chivalry is not dead! A few years ago, my daughter Elissa was dating Ryan, the man who is now my son-in-law. I recall watching Elissa and Ryan leaving our house on a date. Elissa had been dating Ryan for some time, but he did something that men often neglect to do. He walked around and opened her car door. She stepped in and he shut the door behind her. It was automatic and unprompted. That gesture said how he cared for her, how important and special she was to him. Now that they are married, he continues to show her this small but important bit of chivalry. These small gestures are sometimes overlooked by those of us who have been married for a while. However, married women still want a white knight to be there for them and to show them that they are exceptional! One woman said, "It is those little things that I miss. For example, he used to get the umbrella for me when it was raining. Even if he got wet, he wanted to make sure I would not." Chivalry is about caring and making your female companion feel special, a priority in your life.

Romance and chivalry are inseparable. A married couple may see them both start to fade as the years pass. However, your spouse always wants to feel special. Pulling a chair out for her before seating yourself, opening the door for her, these small acts communicate that you value her, that she is special in every way. Men, you must take the lead. Focus again on those little things that your wife appreciated. Talk with her about the pleasures and enjoyments that she likes. Don't be afraid to take the time to understand her and her desire. Remember, this is something that benefits you both. Ladies, when your husbands try to be chivalrous and romantic, praise their efforts. Encourage them to believe in themselves again. It is time now to rekindle the flame of romance.

Men, take a few minutes to review this list of romantic touches that say, "I love you":

- Taking the time to open doors for her

- Holding her hand when you are together in public.

- Leaning over to give her a small kiss in your quiet times together.

- Taking time to look deeply into her eyes so you see the sparkle again. Tell her that you love her.

- Flirting with her, teasing her, enjoying your physical attraction to one another.

- Being openly affectionate toward her, revealing an attitude that cares about her comfort and pleasure.

- Saying the words and showing her in a thousand subtle ways, "I love you!"

Date each other

Dating puts the magic back into a marriage. It will help you to cherish and desire each other again. You may have assumed that because you are married, your dating life is no longer a priority. This is a major misconception. Dating should never leave your relationship. A recent book titled *For Women Only*[1] recorded a notable response concerning American women and men: most men stated that they would prefer to be unloved rather than to be disrespected, the opposite of the preference for women. The implications for your marriage seem clear. Spending time together emphasizes the fact that you love your wife. Dating provides special, unique times together to reconnect. It leads to positive conversations that uplift both of you. Dating is designed to develop closeness and fun in your relationship. (It should not be a time for mutual psychotherapy.). It helps to reprioritize what is important in your relationship. When you schedule dates with your wife, even with a busy schedule, you put away the cares of the world for a few hours to say, "I want to be with you alone."

> **Dating is designed to develop closeness and fun in your relationship.**

In order to reestablish date nights, planning and time are required. Guys, do not expect your wives to do all the preparation. So many things have changed—kids to get ready, babysitters to find, and food to put on the table—so you must help with the preparations if dating is to be a priority again. Divide the responsibilities so that it does not become a job for one person. Make dating a special event. "Special" does not necessarily mean it will require a great deal of money or many hours away from the home. Rather, it means that you will devote some time to doing the things that make your relationship unique and fun.

---

1. Shaunti Feldhahn, *For Women Only* (Sisters, OR: Multnomah Books, 2004).

Romance is a key factor in marriage, even when you are married. Romance for a married couple is like having a love affair forever. It renews the quality of love and physical desire that you have for one another. So often I hear men say there is no need to date anymore because they are already married. How foolish this is! Dating recaptures the intimacy and ardor that you had at the beginning of your relationship. It enables you to find new ways to rekindle the passion and desire in each of you.

For dating to work, the two of you will need to sit down with a calendar and plan times to make this work. I cannot stress enough how important this planning is. Romantic evenings will not just happen. Arrange activities that allow you both to be involved and active. Plan some dates that provide more intimate moments. I recommend that you schedule at least two dates per month and, if possible, more. Have a Plan A (the time and date you know would be best) and a Plan B (an alternative when Plan A does not work due to illness, bad weather, or something else unexpected). Begin with activities that you both enjoy and that do not require a great deal of expense. Some possibilities are:

- Eating a private lunch or dinner by a lake.
- Hiking or walking on a path together with a picnic at the end.
- Sharing a private time by yourselves in the woods.
- Sunbathing by a river or stream in a secluded spot.
- Ice skating.
- Sledding.
- Sipping hot chocolate by a warm fire.
- Cuddling together after watching a movie. (Yes, guys, this may even be a "chick flick.")

- Holding hands as you walk through a museum together.

- Enjoying a candlelit bath together.

As you can see, it does not take much to have an enjoyable date, but it does take planning and preparation. You can have some treasured time with your best friend if you are willing to try.

You seek love. You desire romance. You long for mutual respect. All of those things can be renewed in your marriage if you take time to work together. Praise each other and build each other up emotionally, physically, and spiritually. This will restore the passion in your marriage. You will build the union that you have longed for and kindle a flame that will burn forever!

 Complete the Diagnostic Evaluation on the next page before continuing.

DIAGNOSTIC EVALUATION

1. Does your wife wish you would make more of an effort or place more emphasis on meeting her needs? How often do you check in with her about such desires?

2. Do you regularly exercise to maintain a healthy lifestyle for you and your wife? If not, what steps could you take to begin to do so?

3. Do you fear speaking openly with your spouse about personal issues? If so, why? What would make you more comfortable in speaking about these?

4. When was the last time you took your wife on a real date? (A trip to Wal-Mart does not count, guys.) Did you plan and carry out the details of the date?

5. Men, now is the time. Your mission: plan a date, arrange all the details, and surprise your wife. Remember to take time to process what she likes and enjoys and plan accordingly. (Some of you may need to be ready to dial 9-1-1, should she faint.)

7. ADJUSTING THE THERMOSTAT

7. ADJUSTING THE THERMOSTAT
DEFUSING CONFLICT WITH
APPROPRIATE DECISION MAKING

*"To man belong the plans of the heart, but from the L*ORD *comes the reply of the tongue." —Proverbs 16:1*

Many recent psychological studies reveal that most couples experience struggles along the path of a marriage. Crises and conflicts are inevitable, but how you handle them determines the health and well-being of your marriage. The problems of the past may affect the present stability of your marriage and the foundational base of the marriage itself. How the two of you make decisions has a direct impact on the trust and security you develop and how these will be maintained in your marriage.

Every person has a certain approach to making decisions, which also affects how he or she applies those decisions. How you make a decision independently, as well as together with your spouse, is an important factor determining the strengths and weaknesses of your marriage.

Faulty decisions

Some couples have no good foundation for any type of decision-making process. They have no plan for dealing with problems that arise in their marriage or personal lives. Unfortunately, this is quite common, so I assume that some couples reading this book have no reliable platform for making decisions. Neither of you may have had any role models in your life to help you in this key area, yet decision making affects your basic day-to-day activities, from grocery shopping to where and what you are going to eat today. The decisions you make when considering large purchases, such as a car or a house, or when you make critical career moves, are all influenced by your ability to make appropriate choices. Married couples who weather life's storms effectively are those who cultivate a consistent and appropriate model of decision making. This model must be acceptable to each of you as you proceed to develop your skills of decision making. If you did not develop an effective pattern of decision making while you were single, chances are that you do not have one for your marriage. If so, you have, no doubt, seen frustrations build between the two of you.

In the early years of marriage, decisions may have been almost comical as you wrestled with each issue, even such simple ones as choosing a restaurant. Every couple has experienced a night of driving up and down the main street of their town passing a number of eating establishments because they were unable or unwilling to make a mutual decision about where they will eat. Neither partner wants to disappoint the other, yet neither person wants to be disappointed, either. Some couples go home upset, not eating at a restaurant at all because they cannot make a mutually satisfactory decision about which restaurant to try. We all have been there. At first, it can be funny, but eventually frustration builds. This frustration can carry over into major decisions of your marriage if a solid pattern of decision making is not established. If you do not establish a plan of action, this inability to make decisions in your marriage can lead to self-doubt and mistrust of your spouse.

If you were raised in a family where your parents did not communicate openly when they needed to solve problems, your struggle with basic decision making can be troublesome. Knowingly or unknowingly, we acquire many of our decision-making skills from what we saw in our homes growing up. If Bob saw his father make all the major decisions for the family by himself, Bob will most likely assume that is the way it is done. If Jody saw her mother make all the decisions concerning the children without consulting her husband, Jody will probably continue that pattern in her family. If there was no mutual decision making in your family, you may be at a loss when it comes to knowing how to make decisions jointly with your spouse.

Parents can also do a disservice to their children by not allowing them to make certain decisions on their own. They may think that they do not want their children to go through what they went through. They don't allow their children to openly discuss the pros and cons and come to a decision. These parents make so many decisions for their children that their sons and daughters never truly face their personal problems, which is necessary if children are to develop mature decision-making abilities. Dealing with the consequences

Working together as a couple to make everyday decisions will build depth in the marriage when conflict comes.

of decisions you make early in your life helps to establish a firmer foundation for making decisions as a young adult and as an older, married adult.

A similar problem develops when one spouse was taught appropriate decision-making skills but the other spouse was not. This can result in significant frustration when one spouse has to make all the important decisions in a marriage because the other is not capable of making decisions. Decision making is a skill that can be developed. Each person in the marriage is able to teach and learn from the decision-making strengths and weaknesses of the other. Working together as a couple to make everyday decisions will build depth in the marriage when conflict comes. Couples who avoid taking the time to understand how they can make mutual decisions, and manage the conflict that may arise in the process, will significantly hinder their ability to trust each other when times of serious trouble occur. On the other hand, if you sit down together and learn how to make decisions, you greatly enhance the trust and security required for your marriage. Perhaps you have noticed the weakness that results from poor decision-making skills in your present marriage. This creates insecurity and mistrust in each partner, and feelings of personal inadequacy may develop.

A spouse who has developed a fly-by-the-seat-of-your-pants method of decision making will frustrate the other spouse. Flying by the seat of your pants may work for a while, especially as a single person, but it will not work as a married couple. Remember, you are a team now and you must function together as a team. This is not a time to feel threatened by each other's abilities. It is a time to learn from each other's strengths as you proceed along the course of your marriage. Effective patterns of behavior will add to your marital security as you develop your problem-solving skills together. You will learn to trust each other's judgment. You will learn flexibility, because there will be exceptions to all rules. The trust you gain by taking a team approach to problem solving and decision making will lay a foundation of trust when serious problems arise. The key factor is your oneness in marriage, which we have discussed throughout the previous chapters. The more you are able to practice true oneness when making decisions, the greater freedom you will have when change is needed in your relationship. Once established, a solid pattern of decision making can be modified appropriately as you proceed through life together, because of the trust you have established in your marriage.

Decision-making styles

In order to understand how you make decisions with your spouse, consider the following styles. Take some time to see which style or pattern is most like you. Be open to discussing these with your partner as you both examine the four types presented. Focus on both the positive and negative aspects of each of these styles.

Style I: Goal Oriented

Decision making in this style has a clearly defined goal and objective. A couple that practices goal-oriented decision making is consistent, staying focused on the direction they wish to go. They take care to define their problem clearly and identify the outcome they wish to achieve. They consider the pros and cons of their decision and gather as much information as they can in order to make an appropriate decision. They request input from each other and from others. They pray together about issues and may ask others to pray with them, trying to make the best decision that God would allow. They are open to other opinions and seek to integrate the information that they receive. Then they make a decision based upon the best information they can acquire, and they follow through in an effort to obtain their desired goal.

Style II: Problem Oriented

In this style of decision making, you focus on what you hope to accomplish with a particular decision but have no clear direction for your lives. Consequently, you have little concern about how the outcome of this situation will help or hinder you in the future. Your philosophy is to live one day at a time or take one step at a time and then see what the future holds. However, without a clearly discerned direction for your marriage, you will have difficulty weighing the options presented to you. You listen to others and your spouse for input, but you tend to focus on your own opinion and the solution you devise yourself. Others may see both of you as people who do their own thing, caring little about the counsel of others, so they don't devote much time or prayer to helping you find solutions. The two of you do not spend a great deal of time considering outcomes of the current problem because you just want to get it solved and move on.

Style III: Avoidance

You may practice this style of problem solving if decision making is hard for you. You are afraid of making a poor choice, so you postpone making decisions to the last possible moment and you try to keep all of your options open until that time. You seek information from others, but this only creates more self-doubt and anxiety as various choices are presented to you. Your spouse may become frustrated as you belabor the point so long, because you allow valuable time to be lost as you try to be certain that you make the right choice. Insecurity characterizes the communication between you and your spouse. Trust can be compromised and damaged if this pattern of making decisions continues.

Style IV: Impulsive

Your decision making has no process at all. Like the problem-oriented decision maker, you focus on living day to day and do not want to think about the problems of tomorrow. However, you consider information only if you stumble across it, and you do not go out of your way to ask for help or wisdom. You are passive in your decision making, to the point of letting your decisions be made by default. The frustrations between you and your spouse will be significant. These irritations grow out of your pattern of reluctance to talk about the choices before you or to truly identify your options. Conflicts will arise frequently and are left unresolved. Very little is accomplished when you need to make decisions as a couple, and loose ends become the norm of your life together.

Establish a reliable method

These four styles of decision making, or some combination of them, are present in the majority of marriages. You are likely to see some variation of the four styles within your marriage. Take time to understand what style of decision making you both have been incorporating into your relationship. Your problem-solving style often reflects your own personality as well as family upbringing. Conflict will emerge in your marriage when you do not establish a reliable method for making decisions together. Some decisions, of course, we

> **Conflict will emerge in your marriage when you do not establish a reliable method for making decisions together.**

make on a day-to-day basis with little thought or need for input (e.g., what we wear, what we will have for lunch, when to buy gas for the car). Other decisions require significant deliberation and will reflect what method of decision making you have chosen as a couple. (Refer back to the four types we have discussed.) Decisions that require both spouses' input can only be done well when you sit down together and take time to discuss all of the options. This indicates how healthy your communication truly is.

Listen to and respect one another

Bill and Mary entered counseling because they were having considerable problems communicating in a number of areas. Decision making and conflict resolution were major concerns. Mary stated at the beginning of one session, "My father told me that Bill should always wait and ask others for advice before making big decisions, such as buying a car. He recently told us that the economy was not good right now and it was not the best time to buy a new car, but Bill just did not seem to listen."

"Mary, I have done a great deal of research on this," Bill answered, "and this is a great time to buy a car. Your dad doesn't know everything."

"My father has bought many cars, Bill, and he knows how to handle money. That is something you do not seem to understand."

Bill recoiled in anger, stating, "Maybe you should have married your dad!"

You can see the ramifications of this conversation and how it portrays the decision-making habits of Bill and Mary. As noted earlier, information from others is appropriate and sometimes needed. You must be open to processing information individually as well as together. By the same token, most decisions require reaching your own conclusions as a couple without your family's intervention. Do not show disrespect for your spouse by letting Dad's knowledge trump your spouse's.

Proverbs 18:13 says, "He who answers before listening—that is his folly and his shame." Good communication requires active listening to each other's comments. You both need to understand your partner's point of view without making "Yes, but…" comments. James 1:19 reminds us that "everyone should be quick to listen, slow to speak and slow to become angry." This is never more necessary than in times of decision making, when conflict and differences are likely to occur. A significant challenge arises when you ignore advice from your spouse and others, choosing instead to rely on your own opinion and ideas (styles II and III).

If you are truly seeking God's guidance, you should be able to listen and respond accordingly to worthy advice. Your desire is always to lift each other up in this process. Decision making is one way in which we want to increase our partner's self-esteem, not tear it down. In your marriage, confidence is built one emotional bolt at a time. A good marriage is one in which you take time to listen, weighing information and alternatives, respecting your spouse's opinion even if it does not agree with your family's or your own opinion. You will make some decisions that you later regret, but do not lower yourself to saying, "I knew we should not have done that," or, "I told you that would not work." This only destroys mutual respect and inflicts pain that may linger for years.

We are all imperfect people and we all make mistakes. We can learn from these mistakes if both marriage partners are willing to forgive and not judge. Praying and seeking God's intervention will open your minds to better understand what your spouse may be trying to share, and vice versa. Again, do not keep score of each other's faults and failures. Decision making is complicated, and you need time to build trust and confidence about what you should do. Stay focused on God, who brought you together. He created both of you and knows your shortcomings, and he placed you together as a couple, making you helpmates to one another. You will make some poor choices, but you can learn from them and refocus on the future together. You are both representatives of God himself, so your marriage should be mutually redemptive. Forget your old mistakes, lift your spouse up from defeat, and move ahead together. Blaming and fault-finding serve no redemptive purpose and in no way honor your marriage covenant.

Determine your individual strengths

Several factors affect how well you respond and communicate in problem solving areas. Certain characteristics about each of you will influence how you address various decision-making situations. Consider the following two questions:

Whose personality is better suited to performing basic decision making in the day-to-day operations of your household?

If you have strengths in this area, be willing to take the lead in household decisions (e.g., menu planning, weekly budgeting, shopping). Use your positive strengths to benefit you both. This has nothing to do with who is more intelligent. Simply ask yourselves: Which of us is able to use good common sense in these areas?

Which of you processes solid analytical skills in the area of personal finance, especially when making long-term decisions such as buying a house, car, or other major items?

Which one of you is more adept at business management and keeping finances balanced? One who acts impulsively and is willing to take chances is not the best partner to address long-term financial commitments. A spouse who is cautious and more analytical, giving careful attention to detail, is often better suited to researching major purchases. Then you can both make the right choice based upon the best information. If you are prone to making snap decisions, your response in this area can have disastrous long-term effects. You may overlook potential hazards that can be detrimental to your financial position for years to come. By openly considering your decision-making styles, strengths, and weaknesses, you can work together to make better decisions. Sound financial strategy with open communication will assure that future goals and objectives will be met. God has provided personal gifts to each one of us, and the gift of wise stewardship is one that must be considered in your marriage.

I cannot emphasize enough how important decision making is in your marriage. Work on creating an environment where problems can be addressed quickly and openly as you journey along the path of married life. Take time to review and be honest about your strengths throughout the marriage. At times, one spouse may be better in certain areas, but the other spouse may acquire more knowledge and skill in others. Share your strengths in an appropriate manner so you can both succeed in decision making.

Keep in mind that if something were to happen to you, you would want your spouse to be able to take responsibility for his or her future. You do not want your spouse to be overwhelmed if a debilitating illness or premature death prevents you from participating in key decisions. This may seem somewhat morbid, but I have often counseled people who found themselves in very sad situations because they did not plan for such a contingency. A spouse who never shares knowledge in the area of finances can leave the other spouse in extreme difficulty and

Stay in step with each other, so that at a moment's notice either partner can make a sound decision

depression if sickness or death unexpectedly removes the finance manager. Inform your spouse of progress as well as problems that are taking place in your financial life. Communication allows each of you to deal with the challenges you face. Decision making encompasses all areas in your marriage. Apathy is not an option. By saying that you will get to this eventually, you only create an area of needless vulnerability in your marriage. You should be able to stay in step with each other, so that at a moment's notice either partner can make a sound decision, no matter what the situation or environment.

When looking at major decisions for the future, be proactive. You need to pray and analyze your choices together. God intends for us to be connected in all spheres as a married couple. In order to do this, you must be communicating with your spouse continuously. Decisions about child rearing, career choices, purchases for your children, or changes in the home require special attention by both of you. Know exactly where you are both going.

Ask yourself if God is in the forefront of your decision-making process. Consider the following words from the Scriptures:

> "And whatever you do whether in word or deed, do it all in the name of the Lord Jesus, giving thanks to God the Father through him." (Col 3:17)

> "I can do all things through Christ who strengthens me." (Phil 4:13 NKJV)

> "And my God will meet all your needs according to his glorious riches in Christ Jesus." (Phil. 4:19)

These verses, as well as many others found throughout God's Word, underscore the fact that God has laid the foundation for the decision-making process, especially with respect to our material needs.

Facing conflict

At times, it may seem impossible for the two of you to agree. However, if you are truly seeking God together, he will reveal his will in the resolution of your differences. He promises, "You will seek me and find me when you seek me with all your heart" (Jer 29:13).

No matter how much we hope we can escape conflict in marriage, it will come. You have no doubt experienced many conflicts already. So, how do you handle conflict with your spouse?

Not all conflict is bad or inappropriate. This misconception can lead you to ignore problems when they arise, resulting in more disagreement. You need to identify the issues surrounding your conflict, specifically focusing on why or what is creating the disruption between the two of you. By not addressing discord when it occurs, you disrupt your communication in other areas. It is easy to develop a habit of avoiding discussion of certain sensitive concerns and issues, because you hope to avoid any conflict. But avoidance usually has the opposite result: when conflict finally comes, it is more emotionally charged and difficult to resolve because you have sidestepped your problems for so long.

Your family of origin can have a direct impact on your ability to deal with conflict in marriage; be aware of this when conflict arises. We all want our personal needs met, and as a single person, you had control over that. Basically, how you lived was up to you. Household conflicts for a single person are usually rare, because there is no one but yourself to consider. When you marry, however, your spouse wants his or her needs met as well. If you were an only child, your parents focused on your needs alone. Others may have seen you as a spoiled child, the favorite one, or the little princess. Your parents may not have considered how their undivided attention affected you. If they were able, they may have tried to fulfill your every wish. If so, when you married, you may have assumed that your spouse would attend to your needs in the same way. That is how it is supposed to be, right? Courtship usually does not reveal that such needs will not be met, because each one of you goes overboard to make the other person's needs a priority.

Ken and Sara had this experience. Sara, an only child, often received whatever she wanted from her parents while growing up. Ken came from a very large family and worked to earn any extras that he wanted. Sara and Ken met in college. Sara did not need to work then, as her parents paid for everything. By contrast, Ken worked full time in the summers and continued to work in college, also receiving scholarships for tuition. After meeting at a party, they began dating at the end of their junior year. Ken tried to indulge Sara in whatever she wanted, even when he did not have the means to do so. They never talked much about money, and Sara, having never lived on a budget while growing up, assumed that Ken also could do whatever he wanted. After college, they married, and Ken was able to acquire a good job with decent pay and benefits. However, the job required them to move several hundred miles from Sara's parents. The cost of living was quite a bit higher, and Sara did not work outside the home. She found that staying at home was boring, so she began to spend money for insignificant items. Ken worked longer hours to compensate for Sara's spending habits, but before long, there was not enough money to pay the current bills or the credit-card debt. Ken finally confronted Sara with the need for her to budget money and change her spending habits.

When they arrived for counseling, Sara was very upset. She felt that somehow she had been deceived. Ken felt powerless to keep up with the financial problems that they were experiencing, based upon Sara's credit-card debt. Sara stated, "My father was always able to take care of me. I do not understand why Ken has so much trouble with our finances. He promised before we were married that he would be able to meet all our needs. I feel that he tricked me. I feel like he has lied to me."

This case may seem fairly simple to understand. We could just point out that Sara's spending habits are the problem. However, don't forget that Ken tried to give her anything she wanted before they were married, without discussing the issue of finances. Ken continued to do the impossible while dating, instead of coming to grips with what was real and practical before their marriage took place. He never addressed their true financial state in conversation with Sara before they were married. He kept up a façade instead of being open and honest with Sara, always believing that at some point her financial IQ would change and she would "get it." Ken's fear of losing her kept him from directly confronting the situation, which only worsened the problem. Sara's parents prepared her to expect her husband to continue pampering her as they did. All of them bore some responsibility for the conflict.

Communication is vital

Open communication is another vital component of your ability to deal with conflict in your marriage. You and your mate need to talk openly about each other's needs. What needs can be met, which are impossible to meet, and which needs require some compromise? It is not uncommon for newlyweds to sweep small problems under the rug to avoid conflict. Unmet expectations and annoying habits are never addressed so as not to upset each other. However, when larger problems do arise over time, the couple finds it awkward to discuss

> **Good communication in marriage means that you do "sweat the small stuff."**

them because smaller ones have been avoided. This can ultimately create a breakdown of trust in the marriage. They have built no foundation for conflict resolution.

Good communication in marriage means that you *do* "sweat the small stuff," not that you leave it alone. Retreating from your spouse to pout does nothing to resolve your problems. You must be willing to sit down and discuss problems together, weighing both the pros and cons. Then you can reach a decision or compromise. Compromise is not an admission of defeat. If one spouse has an obviously better solution to a problem, the other spouse should not try to save face. A couple focused on God's will can be open with one another, admitting when they need to change without shame or gloating. God's design of "one flesh" in marriage means that two people work together to become one. In that process, you can minimize conflict if you focus repeatedly on each other's strengths and embrace them.

Learn to compromise

Fellows, let me remind you of the exhortation in Ephesians 5, which calls you to be a servant to your wife and place her needs above your own. This means that you will try to resolve a conflict by arriving at a compromise with which both of you are comfortable. Compromise promotes growth in a relationship as it allows couples the opportunity to freely talk about how they are thinking and feeling. It creates a safe environment where you can disagree without criticism. There should be an openness that builds trust, security, and constructive dialogue.

Conflict can be routinely resolved if you establish a safe environment in your marriage where your words and actions reflect the spirit of Christ. If you do not have such an environment in your marriage, reflect back on the patterns of conflict resolution that you learned from your family. As previously mentioned, these old tapes may cause you to become angry, feel hurt, or withdraw from your spouse whenever differences emerge. You need to examine and work intentionally to change these patterns of dealing with conflict. God wants the best for your marriage, but very often bad habits from the past will haunt you until you identify and deal with them appropriately. This is where Christian counseling can be of great help. If disagreements are very difficult for you and your spouse to handle, but you do not understand why you respond as you do, it is time for you to seek help to resolve these issues.

Myra was raised in a family where her father's work responsibilities took him away from home for most of the week. She was the middle child, with an older sister and younger brother. Her mother had poor health and was seldom able to assist Myra with any of her adolescent needs or projects. However, if Myra raised these personal issues with her father, he would always ask her not to do anything that would upset her mother. Myra stated, "My dad would always say, 'We must think about your mother's health and not put her through any more added stress.' I would just keep my feelings and emotions inside." As a result, Myra felt trapped with her emotions. She felt as if she could never be angry with anyone or about anything. Conflict was to be avoided at all costs. She dated very little in high school and seldom in college, focusing on studies and a career in accounting.

Myra met Tom through a blind date shortly before graduating, and they continued to date after college. He was involved in video production and had a very outgoing personality. Tom had been raised in a family where opinions and emotions were shared openly. Conflict and challenges were a way of life, and Tom had become a passionate debater. Tom said that he could argue with the best of them. Myra was captivated by his charisma and strength. She felt safe in the way he took control of awkward situations and made quick decisions. It all seemed perfect.

Marriage brought many changes, most importantly a new job for Tom and a move far away from any relatives. In the new town, Tom quickly made new friends, but Myra did not. Myra began to feel lonely and neglected. She isolated herself at home, and Tom began to complain about her reclusive behavior. Tom demanded that she get some counseling to deal with "her problem." Coming to counseling seemed like an admittance of failure to Myra. She said, "I must be crazy. I just do not know how to stand up to him. In the beginning, Tom's assertiveness and strength seemed like a safety net for me. Now, he treats me like some kind of enemy, and I am scared of him."

As noted earlier, Myra had learned that conflict was to be avoided at all costs. Every major decision was left up to Tom, even when she did not agree with him. She began to say that he was always right. Any statement of Tom's with which she did not express total agreement would trigger an argument, so she became fearful of expressing her opinions to him. Myra's response to Tom was to isolate herself and retreat from him, which added to his belief that she was the problem in their marriage.

As you read this description, it's clear how Myra arrived at her present behavior. But Tom was accustomed to conflict and liked a good debate. He failed to recognize Myra's insecurity with this manner of dealing with differences, and he did not see the need for him to reassure her of the security of their relationship.

In counseling, Tom stated that he enjoyed their dating and the beginning of the marriage because Myra made him feel special. His wife's admiration made him feel good about himself. Tom said, "She adored my strength and tenacious personality." However, he failed to see that he did not reciprocate. He saw Myra only as an extension of himself. In the beginning of the marriage, Myra's feelings about Tom actually allowed her to voice her opinions and differences with him. However, Tom did not understand that this created an opportunity to build Myra's confidence and break her insecurities about expressing herself. He interrupted Myra often when she tried to state her opinion. Due to his upbringing, Tom saw her outspokenness as a healthy challenge—and the challenge prompted a debate. Then Myra would retreat, which made Tom angry and resentful. He was puzzled by her doormat behavior and could not fathom why she was not more assertive.

Counseling allowed Tom to see what his behavior had destroyed. He sought forgiveness from Myra. This rekindled Myra's desire for Tom. She also felt enabled to express herself again. She became more assertive about her opinions and more open in expressing what she needed in their marriage. For his part, Tom began to see compromise as something positive and acceptable.

Marriage partners who are capable of compromise can build a relationship of personal closeness to each other. It is not a question of winning or losing. Someone with a servant's heart will share needs, listen attentively, and act on what is heard. It is active listening, which reflects back what is heard, aiding understanding, that enables marriage partners to make decisions together. Healthy decision making and conflict resolution build opportunities for the closeness in marriage that was intended by God. Trust, desire, and mutual respect will again be seen as you trust in God and reflect his will in your life through your actions. The words "I love you" will take on a whole new meaning as a sense of genuine security is reborn. Your marriage can work differently if you only take the time to learn new ways to solve problems and resolve your conflicts. Do not think that it is too late. God can and will restore new life to your marriage. Remember Paul's declaration of faith: "I can do everything through him who gives me strength" (Phil 4:13).

I counsel many couples who say, "But it is too late for us. We have grown so far apart." Yet God can work miraculous changes in areas of your life that you thought were impossible, including your marriage. He proclaims, "Call to me and I will answer you and tell you great and unsearchable things you do not know." (Jer 33:3).

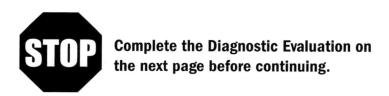

STOP Complete the Diagnostic Evaluation on the next page before continuing.

DIAGNOSTIC EVALUATION

Review together and discuss the following questions regarding your present methods of decision making and conflict resolution:

1. Do you allow your spouse to express differences with you without being defensive or critical? If not, how could you create a safer environment for expressing differences?

2. Do you take time to hear and understand the nature of the differences, truly listening to what your partner is saying? The next time conflict arises, practice active listening to make sure that you understand your spouse's perspective.

3. Are you willing to compromise? If not, why not? Do you see compromise as a failure on your part?

8. RESTARTING THE ENGINE

8. RESTARTING THE ENGINE
DISCOVERING THE DIFFERENCE
BETWEEN SEX AND INTIMACY

"I belong to my lover, and his desire is for me."
—Song of Solomon 7:10

I know this will not surprise you, ladies, but men desire to be sexually intimate with their wives. God created males and females differently in our natures, our personalities, and our needs. He also created us with many similarities. Sexual relations, love, and intimacy can bring great joy to your relationship or great disappointment and hardship. It all depends on understanding the differences and similarities of male and female.

Perhaps you have heard the expression, Men give love to receive sex, while women give sex to receive love. The problem with this statement is that it is a mixture of truth and error. It assumes that men are concerned only with physical pleasure and women only with emotional contentment. Neither alone is true. God made both male and female to be emotional and physical in our love for each other. God specifically created in each gender the ability to be sexually expressive and to desire sexual activity in a manner truly honoring to God. Someone who has a servant's heart can fulfill what God intended in intimacy, sexual expression, and ultimately love. Our goal in marriage should be to minimize our sexual differences and maximize our similarities in order for romance and passion to flourish. This will allow sexual fulfillment and intimacy to become one component in your marriage. Binding these two together will express true love in every way.

Differences between men and women

Before we focus on the similarities of the sexes, let us note some basic differences between men and women. This is not a comprehensive list but one that should help us understand how each gender is unique.

Characteristics of the female

- Needs to be nurtured
- Needs to feel protected
- Needs to feel safe and secure with her partner
- Desires emotional needs to be met
- Is more open to emotional needs
- Is better at expressing emotions outwardly
- Is more openly engaged in dealing with personal issues
- Is more responsive sexually when the whole body is desired, not just parts
- Understands the concept of nurturing
- Likes to be cuddled and snuggled to create a feeling of being safe
- Wants a safe environment in order to express emotional and sexual needs

Characteristics of the male

- Is less focused on feelings

- Is more visually stimulated

- Is more physically focused: touch is important

- Often finds it hard to express emotions

- Is unsure how to share feelings

- Is often competitive in areas that females may view as adolescent

- Needs to know he is respected

- Needs to be admired for his ideas and skill

- Often appears more concrete in thought, more black and white in his thinking

These are only a few of the differences between men and women, but knowing these may help you explore aspects of your sexual relationship that have been inadequate. This is not to say that the above lists are exclusive to only one sex, but they will help you to understand how you and your spouse perceive these areas of sex and intimacy.

God intended sex to be pleasurable and for intimacy to bond you emotionally with your spouse.

With busy jobs, schedules, and families to care for, a couple can often feel robbed of a healthy sexual relationship. Sex often becomes a routine experience, rather like bowling night. It may lose the excitement and passion it once had in your life. The playfulness of sexual relations can be lost or diminished. Again, note that Scripture says God intended sex to be pleasurable and for intimacy to bond you emotionally with your spouse. Proverbs 5:18 directs a husband to see his wife's body like a fountain to be blessed and enjoyed.

Proverbs 5:19 goes on to say, "May her breasts satisfy you always, may you ever be captivated by her love." Likewise, "the wife of your youth" is directed to satisfy her husband. Making love should be exciting, something to anticipate. It should not become just another recreational activity. The goal is to please each other and become a master of lovemaking with your spouse. The goal is to bring true lovemaking back to your relationship, not just to have sex.

Has lovemaking become a chore for you and your spouse? Has it become boring? If you answered yes to either question, read on.

Restoring and renewing your sex life

As we've seen several times, "one flesh" is God's purpose for your marriage. You expressed that purpose when you exchanged your marriage vows. A stable union between the two of you must exist. In order to have spiritual and emotional union with your spouse, physical union is imperative, and it must be a union that excludes all others. Proverbs 5:15 directs the husband to "drink water from your own cistern, running water from your own well." The implication of this direction is clear when we apply it to lovemaking. The physical relationship with your spouse should be refreshing and cleansing. It should be an act of renewing your mate, not polluting or corrupting your mate. It is an abandonment of your needs to meet the needs of your spouse. A husband is first to make sure that his wife is pleased with every aspect of lovemaking before seeking his own sexual gratification. It involves taking time to know each other again or maybe for the first time. Consider the following:

> "All night long on my bed I looked for the one my heart loves." (Song of Solomon 3:1)

> "May your fountain be blessed, and may you rejoice in the wife of your youth. A loving doe, a graceful deer—may her

breasts satisfy you always, may you ever be captivated by her love." (Proverbs 5:18–19)

The Scriptures are clear: husbands and wives are to know and find pleasure in each other's bodies. Sexuality is God's gift to couples, but it must be tempered by an understanding of the needs and expectations we each have, both physically and emotionally. Men and women are different regarding sexual intimacy and sexual pleasure. Exploring these differences openly will lead to a better understanding of each other's needs and desires. Over time, this communication may have been lost between the two of you. Now is the time to reclaim your passion for one another by rediscovering the beauty of lovemaking with your spouse.

Communication

I have mentioned various communication issues throughout this book, but now let us consider some key aspects of communication that are often forgotten in lovemaking, such as listening, sharing, and touching.

Listening

To better understand each other when addressing the sexual aspect of your relationship, you must practice the art of listening. Susan sat in my office frankly stating that she had never been satisfied sexually with John in their marriage. "He never takes time to make sure I am stimulated or satisfied when it comes to lovemaking," she said. "He only thinks about himself. Over the years, I have learned just to get through it with John."

I asked Susan when she had last tried to talk to John about her frustrations. She responded, "I don't know. Several years ago, I guess. It is just not worth it. It just creates an argument when I bring it up. He is never sensitive to my needs."

In order for such a relationship to change, each partner must be willing to reexamine the sexual desires and motivations of the other. They must genuinely listen to one another in order to facilitate change together. At the beginning of the training to become professional counselors, new students are taught to be attentive and sensitive to communication by being active in their listening skills. They must make sure that they truly hear and understand what someone is saying. They must clarify what the other person is saying in order to comprehend the message and thus enable a proper response. Couples must learn this important skill, specifically in the sexual arena.

Men want to "get to the bottom line" and may disregard what another person says en route to that point.

Unfortunately, men frequently have poor listening skills. Why? Men want to "get to the bottom line" and may disregard what another person says en route to that point. Listening means keeping your thoughts and opinions silent until you understand what the other person is trying to tell you. This is especially true when discussing sexual relations with your wife. You need to ask for clarification as she describes her sexual needs and desires to make sure you understand what she is asking for. Pay close attention to her "I" statements, which allow her to take ownership of her wants and needs. Here are some examples of "I" statements in such a conversation:

I need you to...
I feel stimulated when you...
I feel more desire when...

Ask any questions you have about what your spouse is sharing. You may need clarification if you don't understand what is being requested. This is not a time to be critical or defensive, or to act as if you understand when actually you do not. It is easy to misinterpret what your partner is saying. You are trying to get to know each other again. You are trying to understand and learn about your spouse's sexual desires so that both of you can enjoy your times of physical intimacy. That requires a new perspective on your relationship, so put aside your assumptions from the past. Focus on your love for the individual in front of you and how you want the very best for him or her in your lovemaking. Effective communication takes time and practice, especially when you are trying to talk about sensitive issues that you may never have discussed at all. You may have been married for many years, but you have to recalibrate your listening skills from time to time so that each of you can continue to learn how your relationship is changing. Talking openly with one another will create a new closeness between you. Although this chapter revolves around your sexual relationship, the closeness that you develop in this area with open communication will blend into all areas of your relationship.

Sharing
You need time to facilitate this kind of dialogue. As noted earlier, you may have lost a high degree of satisfaction because your lovemaking has become a routine exercise. Knowing your differences and understanding how those differences affect each partner's desire will enhance your experience. This process of rediscovery should continue your entire life. As a psychologist, I am greatly surprised by how many couples have been married for years yet have never expressed to one another what feels sexually satisfying to them.

In some situations, physical health can impair or diminish lovemaking and sexual drive. Amanda and Paul struggled for a number of months because of Amanda's physical problems, which had intensified to the point where lovemaking had become very painful and almost impossible. She had sought help from various doctors, but each one identified a medical condition that could not be cured. When they came to see me, Amanda had stopped all sexual contact with her husband out of fear of failure. Paul had responded by pulling away emotionally and physically, frustrated that he could not express his sexual desire for Amanda. He felt as if he had to repress any sexual overtures whatsoever. When Amanda and Paul began to speak about the issues, Amanda told me that she was a total failure and that Paul deserved much better. The following conversation took place.

"Tell me, Amanda, why do you feel you are a total failure now?" I asked.

"I can't have any type of sexual involvement with Paul. I can't perform. I am just worthless," she said.

"Well, you say you can't have sexual intercourse, but what about responding with other kinds of physical touch—such as holding, caressing each other, or stimulating one another. Are these things possible, Amanda?"

"I have thought about this a number of times," she said, "but it would just be a tease for Paul, not fulfilling at all what he wants."

I turned to her husband and said, "Paul, is that how you feel?"

Looking very startled, Paul responded, "Are you kidding?! I would love to do those things, holding and caressing, just touching. Any type of intimate touching is what I need and desire. Yes, intercourse would be great, but having any touch—being able to hold her in some way—is something I have longed for. Amanda just seemed so overwhelmed with everything that I never knew how to approach her."

Amanda exclaimed, "Paul, you mean you have wanted to do this for a long time? I was so afraid. I thought that if I approached you, you would just think of me as being half a woman. Why didn't you say something to me?"

Paul said he hadn't told her this because he feared rejection. Both had wanted greater physical intimacy for years, but poor communication and insecurity had stopped them from being open with each other.

This happens more often than you might think. Talking openly with one another about these problems is essential if you are going to grow close again. Such conversations may uncover other areas in your marriage that require time to reflect. Are you prepared to do this? Ask yourself what you really desire in this area. If you trust God, he will give the strength and courage to become open and vulnerable in your communication. By being able to discuss what is taking place in your sexual relationship, you can begin a new chapter of your marriage together.

I can't tell you how many married men and women I have counseled over the years who never "got the details." Most often, the problem was their embarrassment in asking candid questions of their mate. Some married couples feel afraid, silly, or stupid about asking the questions they need to ask. Men can find this extremely difficult, but the same can be true of women. Poor information, lack of information, or no information has led to many an unsatisfactory wedding night, wedding weeks, and entire marriages. I often hear the problem described like this:

Some married couples feel afraid, silly, or stupid about asking the questions they need to ask.

"Dr. Vaughn, we have been married now for eight years and I find intercourse so painful and undesirable."

"So what has your family physician said about this pain? What help or referral has he been able to provide?"

"I really never went into much detail with him about this. It was just too embarrassing."

"So in eight years you have never explained to your doctor what was taking place?"

"Well, I tried but...no."

Intercourse for this woman had been so painful that she finally asked her husband to stop, telling him that she just did not enjoy it. Not wishing to physically hurt her, the husband just resigned himself to the belief that the problem could not be remedied. They did not discuss it with a physician because of their embarrassment. As it turned out, the problem was easily treated and could have been solved years previously.

That conversation actually took place in my office. The wife had never talked to her physician about her pain. There had been a lack of vaginal lubrication during intercourse from the very beginning of their marriage. The pain was almost unbearable, yet she had never tried to discuss this with anyone. I asked if she had asked for advice from the women around her, at the church or office. She again stated that she was too embarrassed to ask. When she did try to talk vaguely with some of her close friends, they just assumed that she did not like sex. This professional woman had a business degree and was part owner of a business. She had three children and was thirty-eight years old.

Yes, poor information leads to poor sexual relations and perpetuates avoidable problems. You can keep these problems to a minimum if you discuss them openly with each other, a physician, or other people that you can trust. I know it may seem embarrassing, but a good physician will answer your questions if you ask. Openly speaking with your spouse gives you an opportunity to describe what feels good and what doesn't feel good, what excites you and what creates pleasure. If you are to have closeness and intimacy in your marriage, you must be willing to discuss your sexual problems and be willing to make any changes that are needed.

Remember, sexual problems affect both men and women. Many men have a faulty knowledge of lovemaking that they never discuss with anyone. Men, it's okay not to know. *It is not okay to remain ignorant.* Many of the problems related to erectile dysfunction are related to the fear of performing inadequately. These mental head games can destroy a good sex life if not discussed openly. And, ladies, the same goes for you: ignorance and embarrassment must be overcome.

Now take time to review your marriage for possible deficiencies in your sexual relationship. Your discussion can start with these two important questions:

1. What do you want or desire in your lovemaking?

2. How can you better communicate your desires to your spouse?

Take time to complete each of the following statements as a way of answering the questions above. Allow yourself to be vulnerable, even if critical statements are made. As always, this is not a competition. You are on the same team, desiring to achieve the same end.

*   I love you most when…

*   The best sexual contact with you is…

*   I feel very sexually aroused when…

*   Intimacy for me is when…

*   When I desire you sexually, I am thinking…

*   I often feel less desirable when…

*   I feel upset most often when…

*   I am most comfortable with you sexually when…

*   I am least comfortable with you sexually when…

The last two statements involve exploring what is most exciting for you sexually and what dampens your desires sexually. This requires a great deal of openness with your spouse. Answer the following questions personally before asking for your spouse's answers:

*   What do I wish you understood about me sexually that would increase my desire to be with you more?

- What do I think intimacy means to my spouse?

- What do I desire for us as a couple—sexually, emotionally, physically, and spiritually?

- Do I have feelings of guilt concerning some kinds of sexual contact with my spouse, and if so, why?

- During childhood, did I get the impression that any sexual behavior was dirty, wrong, or unbiblical?

- Do I find it uncomfortable to talk about any of these things?

- What creates sexual arousal for me?

- What could increase sexual pleasure for me?

These questions allow you to shape your future lovemaking. Healthy communication is critical for sexual enjoyment. Sex without open communication becomes little more than a physical exercise that finally loses the spontaneity and pleasure that God intended. Effective communication will help both of you to meet each other's sexual needs, allowing for a more fulfilling sex life and true intimacy.

Men remember that your wife is not aroused by grabbing her breasts and asking if "she wants to do it." Your wife is special; treat her with respect and dignity at all times. If your actions and language make sex seem dirty or cheap, you will lose her respect.

Physical touch

The degree to which you find various kinds of physical touches pleasurable will have a significant impact on your physical desire for one another. Take time to discuss the following types of physical touching. Talk about what feels good for each of you and what does not:

- Holding hands

- Hugging

- Caressing

- Light kissing

- Passionate kissing

- Physical stimulation while clothed

- Physical stimulation while nude

- Full-body massage

- Manual stimulation

- Sexual intercourse

- Oral stimulation

This discussion can be uncomfortable if it triggers memories of past difficulties. If this begins for either of you, take time to discuss the following question: *Do you find that discussing sexual intimacy and physical touching is something that you desire, or is this discussion simply another task to be done?*

If you continue to view your sexual relationship as a task or performance, then you must look at why you view sexual encounters this way. As has been discussed, many women say the excitement, intimacy, and enjoyment of lovemaking is gone and has been replaced by a need to perform. How sad this is! God never intended sexual relations to be a job or just an act to perform. As is stated in the Song of Solomon, lovemaking is to be something to delight in and an enjoyment of true pleasure for you both. Share your expectations in the area of lovemaking with your spouse. What

Many women say the excitement, intimacy, and enjoyment of lovemaking is gone and has been replaced by a need to perform.

is your ideal sexual experience? What would be the appropriate setting, climate, or environment to find more pleasure with your spouse?

These are all questions that when answered together fulfill sexual pleasure in the way God intended. Men, take time to build your wife's confidence by letting her help you know how to explore and enjoy her body. Be compassionate and tender, focusing on her and not you. Understand her emotions. Do not focus just on the physical desires and responses. More than once in counseling, I have heard wives say to their husbands, "I want you to focus on me during sex, not just my breasts." Viewing your wife as the one that God has chosen for you and holding her in high esteem will awaken a new desire and response in her. Sharing on this level of intimacy will bring a closer walk with her like never before. Sharing and listening are the keys to unlocking this intimacy, to achieving the closeness that you are both looking for and the sexual openness you want.

I mentioned earlier that couples will often come into counseling after several years of marriage saying that "the spark or fire is gone." What is needed to restart the flame that will rekindle the fire that you so long for? We know that sexual feelings can change after a few years of marriage. Hopefully, you can see the need for a more mature love. By the discussions that now will take place regarding sharing of needs, emotional and sexual response, and desire to be with each other, a more mature love will begin to grow. Romance and passion can grow and mature like never before through the openness you now both have together. Begin by placing your spouse back in the position needed—best friend and soul mate. The foundational pieces of your marriage have been reviewed, reconciled, restored, and now need to be reestablished. The previous pages have revealed the foundational pieces needed to reestablish sexual closeness, vulnerability, and intimacy. Now plan to make it part of your marriage.

Have a plan

I know it can be awkward to schedule a time to be together sexually. I am not saying that you have to sit down and literally say, "On Friday the 24th, at 1:00 PM, we are going to have sex." This would be foolish. However, in a day of busy schedules and numerous conflicting commitments, lovemaking seems to have fallen to the bottom of the list of priorities for many couples. You may feel that scheduling a time for intimacy will take away from the romance and passion. On the contrary, it can often build romance. There can be an amount of anticipation for both of you. Little notes or romantic comments may fuel the fire when the moment arrives. You can make the scheduling romantic and fun.

Knowing that there are certain times each week when they can look forward to sexual encounters will truly enhance a couple's sexual desire and drive. It will allow you the joy of focusing on each other instead of just grabbing the remnants of time left over. If you allow adequate time for sexual encounters, you can have adequate sexual foreplay in the process. (Yes, foreplay is a necessary component of lovemaking.) Guys, you can take the opportunity to start foreplay days ahead through her sense of hearing or touch. Just a light touch on the neck as you tell her you're looking forward to Thursday afternoon awakens sexual alertness (done at the right moment, of course).

Again, men, focus first on your wives' desires. For your wife, foreplay can actually start long before you enter the bedroom. It begins with your tenderness for her throughout the day. It may even be the fact that you helped her with some task when she really needed you before she even asked. It may be a long hug when you get home. Realize, men, that women actually enjoy the act of intimacy longer than we do. This enjoyment should begin before and after the actual act of intercourse. Ladies, cultivate your husband's sexual appetite. Communicate openly your desire to be with him sexually. He needs to know that you enjoy making love to him and that you find not only pleasure but also security when you are with him.

Remember, the Bible clearly states that the marriage bed is undefiled. But marital needs for sex are only met when you both feel at ease. Talk openly with one another about sexual techniques, positions, and so on, but focus only on what is advantageous for both of you. Never bully your mate to perform something that is not safe or not pleasurable. Song of Solomon 2:3–7 suggests that a couple will need to be quite candid in telling one another what is pleasurable, arousing, and stimulating. It is all right to experiment, but the key must be that you both feel contented in doing so.

Below are some questions to help you start a discussion and to aid you in exploring areas of sexual arousal that could possibly help break you out of ruts.

- What do you feel comfortable with regarding sexual positions?

- Are you willing to change the environment where we have sexual encounters?

- What surroundings bring you pleasure (e.g., lights, candles, satin sheets)?

- Would you be willing to try massages, using creams and lotions? (Try things that are very sensuous, such as candies, honey, and whipping cream. Although this seems silly for some couples, it can be very exciting and fun for others.)

- For the woman: Would you be willing to try new lingerie or other items of clothing that may be sexually stimulating?

- For the man: Would you experiment with colognes and various perfumes which are sensuous and add sexual excitement?

- Could we add flowers, rose petals, or aromatic spices to the bedroom or bed?

- What kind of music do you find most arousing?

This list is by no means complete, but it may help you begin to discuss how to enhance your sexual pleasures. Let me again restate the need for fun and pleasure in your sex life. God intended a married couple's sexual behavior to be pleasurable. It is time now to rekindle and develop a closeness in your sex life. Talk openly and honestly about what works and what does not for you. The key is enjoyment, and whatever brings enjoyment is for the two of you to discover.

Say no to pornography

However, I warn you, do not to tempted to use pornography (print or video) in an effort to enhance the pleasure of your marriage bed. Pornography has no place in your bedroom or in your life. It only opens the door for lust, deceit, and mistrust in your marriage. *Pornography can destroy your trust and respect for each other, now and in the future.* Stay away from it.

 **Complete the Diagnostic Evaluation on the next page before continuing.**

DIAGNOSTIC EVALUATION

---

1. Your assignment is to review and discuss the questions listed in this chapter. Take the time to truly understand your sexual needs and those of your wife.

2. Men, take the time now to set the stage for a better sex life by refocusing on making your wife feel special again. Sexual foreplay begins at the beginning of the day, not at bedtime. Meeting her needs will bring her back to yours.

9. SALVAGING THE TRANSMISSION

9. SALVAGING THE TRANSMISSION
SAVING YOUR MARRIAGE
FROM AN EXTRAMARITAL AFFAIR

"Serve wholeheartedly as if you were serving the Lord, not men, because you know that the Lord will reward everyone for whatever good he does." —Ephesians 6:7–8

You may have faced what seemed like insurmountable problems in your marriage. At such times, it appears as if the mountain you are trying to climb is too high and cannot be conquered. Marriage takes work, and some marital problems require superhuman work. It might appear easier just to quit, but do not be discouraged: God states that he has begun a good work in you both (remember, you are "one flesh" now), and he will continue his work if you are just faithful and look to him (Phil 1:6).

Extramarital affairs are particularly challenging, and you both may wonder if there is any way to salvage your marriage after such an experience. Indeed, extramarital affairs break many marriages. However, a Christian couple can draw upon supernatural resources to overcome this marital emergency. The first key to overcoming this problem is to remain focused on your spouse only. This is difficult, considering the temptations that we experience on a daily basis in environments that entice us to reach for something new. Such temptations are especially alluring when problems in our own marriages appear to be too hard to overcome.

Men, I again challenge you to be very careful to control your eyes and thoughts when you feel distant from your wife. They can easily wander to the colleague in the next office, the woman just down the production line from you, or the neighbor next door. Your imagination will convince you that she is so sweet, caring, and lovely in appearance. The conversation seems innocent. No harm in talking, right! Before long you like talking to her more than your wife. You find ways, excuses, to be around her. You forget what is real or fantasy. Your desire for this woman may bring new excitement, but it will bring no peace. "I could talk to her so much easier than Joan," Mike said. "I did not start out to have an affair. Home just had so much conflict, and we always seem to be at odds. When I met Michelle, she was just more open with me. She listened, laughed, and joked with me. That is something that Joan stopped doing a long time ago. It seemed as if God had brought somebody wonderful into my life."

Deceitful excitement

This excitement of an extramarital relationship is deceitful. It carries a price that you will regret, a price that affects more people than you can imagine. Proverbs 5:8–10 says that when you enter the house of another woman who is not your own wife, you lose all that you hold dear.

> Keep to a path far from her,
>   do not go near the door of her house,
> lest you give your best strength to others
>   and your years to one who is cruel,
> lest strangers feast on your wealth
>   and your toil enrich another man's house.

In Matthew 5:28, Christ states clearly that to look upon another woman with lust in your heart is equivalent to the act of adultery. I know you may feel angry and frustrated about the problems in your marriage. You may believe that I do not understand the disconnect in your marriage and the loneliness you feel. But the person God has entrusted you with—this wife that you now have—is the one that he intended for you. Your struggles may seem great, but an intimate relationship with another woman will not provide the answer you seek. You need to break free of the lie of adulterous temptation and refocus on your wife.

Ladies, this is just as true for you. Resolving your marital struggles will take time. Realize the temptations that your husband may face. Look at what is taking place in your own life to see what you can change in order to help him. I invite you to lift up your husband in what he may be facing daily. If your communication together has been open, then these problems may be foreign to you. However, if your husband is distant and disconnected in conversation, he may be deeply involved in a struggle with lustful thoughts and desires for someone else who "understands him."

Contemporary novels, movies, and soap operas suggest that you can live a double life, but it is impossible.

An affair may seem normal in today's society. Contemporary novels, movies, and soap operas suggest that you can live a double life, but it is impossible. You may even try to justify your behavior because of sexual problems at home. You may rationalize that it is okay because, in many ways, your extramarital affair is keeping things balanced so you can stay in your marriage. But be sure of this: It is never appropriate to cheat on your wife or husband. Never does the Bible condone these actions. No matter what your friends or co-workers may tell you, an affair will not help you deal with the problems and frustrations at home. Your marriage was intended to satisfy all your needs and desires for human companionship.

Divergent paths

Affairs happen most often when we fail to consider the destination of various paths that we choose throughout our lives. When the paths of marriage partners start to change and you find that the two of you are going down two different roads—parallel tracks, with no cross over—then problems will abound. If you both shut down emotionally and do not attempt to understand your struggles, you will create an opening for someone else to step into your place. Someone will be willing to listen and help your spouse with the problems you no longer seem to care about. Men, if you are too busy because of your friends, recreational activities, or work, you can be sure that there is another man somewhere (at that soccer game, at school, or at work) who is willing to listen to your wife's emotional pain. He will be willing to tend to her wounded heart. Ladies, when you are too busy to listen, play, or engage with your husband, you can be sure that some woman at work or at the basketball practice will do these things that make him feel wanted and desired. We all fear rejection and abandonment, similar to a child lost and alone in a store. Feeling alone or unloved leads to resentment. Resentment can build if you do not take the time to consider the path you and your spouse are on, making sure that you are traveling one road and not two. This careful reflection requires both of you to stop and observe the warning lights on the marital dashboard.

Sitting in my office, Bill stated that he had become involved in an extramarital affair because this woman listened and cared about what he was struggling with. He and his wife Virginia had conversations all right, but they always focused on the kids, her mother, her self-image, her health. He had tried to listen and help Virginia, but as the years passed, it seemed as if she had more needs than he could handle. Intimacy and sex were a bother to her. She always seemed tired and not interested. When he tried to initiate a conversation about having some fun together, she had more pressing concerns. Bill kept hoping that things would change and get better. However, his frustrations increased, his resentments grew, and before long, bitterness filled his heart. He and Virginia seemed to quarrel about anything, and he learned to just give in. Bill said that he felt as if he was in a trap.

"I felt like her kid," Bill said. " She was always correcting me. 'Wrong word, Bill.' 'Sit up, Bill.' 'Do not be grouchy, Bill.' I just shut down, Dr. Vaughn. I was just done."

Before long, Bill said, he did not care to come home; it was just easier to stay at work. During this period of disconnect from Virginia, he met Kay. It was an innocent relationship at first, or so he thought. She was lonely like Bill, and their mutual loneliness seemed to push them together. "We could talk about our frustrations, and before long we found we could laugh and even help each other to be optimistic," Bill said.

You can see from the above example how subtle the openings to temptation become when you and your spouse do not deal with frustrations in your marriage. These openings point you or your spouse away from shared emotions. You focus more and more on understanding and learning about the needs of this new person instead of trying to be involved with your spouse. Before long, you feel you have a closer connection with this new person than you ever had with your spouse. You begin to tell yourself that this is what you have longed for and needed. You justify this new relationship because "you deserve to be happy."

Mary said to me, "I was just lonely. Bob would always be gone, staying away so much that I felt as if I did not really matter. It was innocent at first when I would talk to Tom. At church, he just seemed nice, loving, caring, and fun. He always seemed to be involved with people on a personal level, and before long, he was talking and listening to me. He would call me during the day to just 'check up on me.' Before long, he opened up a part of my heart that had not been touched for years. He cared."

Mary said she remembered a time when Tom brought her a flower that he had picked along the side of the road because the beauty of it reminded him of her. She said that Bob had not brought her flowers or done anything of this nature for years. She began to meet with Tom at a local coffee shop, just to talk about biblical things. It was not long before she was enmeshed with this individual and wanted to leave Bob.

Affairs can be broken

I offer these illustrations to make you think critically about any problems in your marriage. Conflicts and challenges abound. The day-to-day struggles of marriage can be monumental, but looking into a new face is not the answer to your problems. You can deal with the battles that you face together, but not if you engage in an affair. If you will both take the time to reexamine the purpose of your marriage and openly discuss the exercises in this book, you will see clearly that the answer to your struggles lie to reconnecting to your spouse, not disconnecting. Affairs can be broken and marriages can be restored. If you have fallen into an extramarital affair and you feel that this other person is your only answer, if you believe that God has provided this new person for you, it is all a lie and fantasy. God has promised relief for your marriage problems, but not with someone new outside your marriage. Finding that relief will take time, and it must be something you are motivated to pursue with forgiveness in your heart and a firm commitment to your wife, not a mistress.

> The day-to-day struggles of marriage can be monumental, but looking into a new face is not the answer to your problems.

"I deserve happiness" is a popular statement these days, but God never said that. God provides contentment, which in time will restore happiness. Isaiah 26:3 states, "You [God] will keep in perfect peace him whose mind is steadfast, because he trusts in you."

By placing your faith back in God and asking him for encouragement, you will find him redirecting your path back to your spouse. He will reconnect the union of your hearts, creating closeness and intimacy again. No matter how troubled your marriage may appear, your marriage can work. In order for this to happen, you must focus on each other, no one else.

Due to the pain and difficulty involved with an affair, it is extremely important to seek professional help not only for your marriage but for yourself. If you are the victim of an extramarital affair, you need help to deal with the hurt. If you are the one who has strayed, you must learn new ways of coping with your problems so this will never happen again. The assistance of a wise pastor or Christian friend is beneficial, but this is a situation where professional Christian counseling may be needed.

At times, the road to recovery from an affair will be extremely painful and difficult to walk. Counseling will aid greatly in the healing process, especially when you are working on forgiveness and reconciliation. Be open with your spouse and resolve to move forward together in trying to remove the pain and hurt. Don't give up. Nothing is impossible when God is working in you and your marriage.

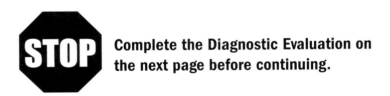 **Complete the Diagnostic Evaluation on the next page before continuing.**

DIAGNOSTIC EVALUATION

Use the following as a checklist to evaluate your vulnerability to an extramarital affair.

1. Do you feel disconnected from your wife? Are you critical of her without appropriate reason?

2. Do you find your thoughts focusing on other women around you at work, at church, at the gym?

3. Have you ventured into a relationship with another woman because you just want to be a "good friend"?

4. Are you involved on an emotional level with a woman other then your wife?

5. Have you or are you presently making phone calls, sending text messages, or sending e-mail messages to another woman, or women, without your wife's knowledge? If she heard these conversations or read the texts, would she be devastated?

6. Are you justifying your behavior with "I deserve to be happy"?

7. Do you feel angry or disconnected from God?

8. Are you willing to seek help to restore your marriage?

If you find yourself answering yes more often than no, heed the warning lights. Take the steps outlined in this chapter to pull back from the temptation; begin to practice the principles laid out in chapters one through nine. I strongly encourage you to seek professional help in restoring your marriage if you cannot break the cyle. Your marriage can be restored!

10. SCHEDULING ROUTINE MAINTENANCE

10. SCHEDULING ROUTINE MAINTENANCE
KEEPING IN TUNE WITH QUALITY TIME, DESIRE, AND CONSISTENCY

"Make my joy complete by being of the same mind, maintaining the same love, united in one spirit, intent on one purpose."
—Philippians 2:2 NASB

Reconnecting with each other again and fulfilling your mutual desires in marriage have been major themes of this book. The foundational values we have discussed—trust, security, and respect—are essential to your marriage. The crucial message has been that both of you can learn how to provide these values and reinforce them in your relationship. We have considered many ways to redirect your focus back to each other in order to feel secure in your love. All of these ideas could be distilled into a single question: "Honey, do you love me?"

At this point, I suspect that every husband is playing the following tape in his mind: *Well, of course, I love you. I have been there for you. I have told you over and over again. Why must we go over this again?* As one man said to his wife in a counseling session, "I told you I loved you a week or so ago. Isn't that enough?"

Guys, that is not enough. Your wife needs to hear and to know that the man she dated, who took time to make her feel secure years ago, is still there for her and only her. You need to learn again how to express romantic love for your mate. Security, trust and mutual respect must also be solid in your marriage. These values will link the two of you together forever. When they are present, you can firmly and unequivocally answer the question, "Do you love me?" In fact, your wife won't need to ask it because the reality of your love will be self-evident.

Express love daily

As the flame of love begins to grow again in your marriage, it will permeate the cold that may have been present for some time. It will generate forgiveness and restoration in both you, taking away the darkness and restoring joy to your relationship. But you must start expressing appreciation of your spouse through words and actions each day. Begin to show that you are focused on your spouse's needs, along with a new understanding and willingness to meet those needs. The spouse before you wants time with you. Your partner needs to be noticed. He or she needs to be understood and respected. As time moves along in marriage, it is easy to forget to do the simple things that daily express love to each other. Now is the time to reestablish those simple habits; everyday acts of love and appreciation for your spouse are essential. Do it with an intensity of devotion that leaves no question as to how much you desire and are willing to change. Simple expressions of love make a huge difference in a marriage. Let me illustrate with a situation that took place early in my career.

> **It is easy to forget to do the simple things that daily express love to each other.**

Growing up in the Midwest, I was always taught to be friendly when meeting new people. I was about twenty-five years of age and new to counseling when I met with a married woman in her early forties who felt she had become invisible to her husband. She felt neglected by him, as if he cared little for her needs or wants. She said he was a Christian man, but he seemed to have lost the desire to be relationally connected with her. She wept openly, believing she had lost her best friend. She came to those counseling sessions very appropriately dressed, hair neatly styled, and completely professional. I believe it was on her second visit that I noticed she wore a perfume with a very pleasant fragrance. It was a fragrance that my wife had tried recently in the department store, and I had asked my wife to remember the perfume because I thought it smelled good. I offhandedly stated to my client as she was leaving how nice her perfume smelled. Bingo! She was so appreciative that I had noticed her perfume. Her last comment was that she wished her husband would take time to notice things like her new perfume. I thought how unfortunate for this woman, as she was looking for the smallest sign of affection from her husband.

My innocent comment had unexpected consequences. When she arrived the next week for her appointment, it was as if she had taken a bath in that new perfume. The fragrance was so strong that I found it difficult to breathe. She was elegantly dressed, as if she were going to an opera. Perhaps you have heard of the counseling term *transference*. This describes a situation in which a person seeks to satisfy an emotional need or desire by looking to someone else because the need is being met by this person; often, the client doens't realize what is taking place. I had noticed her perfume. My offhand comment had reinforced her desire for someone to take notice of her, so she exaggerated the features that I had praised.

She was not a mentally unbalanced woman. She was a Christian woman who sincerely yearned for someone to notice her. As I began to gently discuss what had happened as a result of my comment, she began to cry. She had not intended to be inappropriate in her actions toward me, but the casual comment of a young man made her feel special again. She had hoped this type of comment would come from her husband's own lips, but the words never came.

Her husband eventually came to the counseling sessions with her. He was a good man who had become so involved in work and hobbies that he had forgotten about the needs of his wife. Let me say it again: He was not a bad guy. In counseling, he began to describe the neglect that he had experienced in his own life. He had become so absorbed in his own activities that he had forgotten to express appreciation for the woman who had made him feel special, his wife. He had actually noticed the new perfume and was going to tell her, but he just never got around to it. As I again related the story of the perfume in a session with both of them, his wife began to weep openly. As her tears dropped to the floor, something incredible happened—he began crying too. He dropped to his knees in front of his wife and, broken in spirit, asked for her forgiveness. Both of them sat sobbing in my office for several minutes. They resolved to renew their commitment to love and cherish each other again. The husband said that he wanted to be the servant he had not been for a long time and to honor his wife in every way possible.

I would like to tell you that I see positive results like this again and again, but many times that is not the case. Instead of forgiveness, it is so easy for the neglected spouse to become bitter and start to blame the other person for the problems. Godly men and women need to look into their own hearts, strip out the pride and arrogance that has taken hold, and allow God to replace it with a servant's spirit. This kind of spirit compels a spouse to kneel in front of a wife or husband and say, "I am sorry. I want to do better, and I want to do it God's way." That repentant attitude can rekindle hope, even in a deeply broken marriage.

Ladies, although I have addressed much of this book toward men, note that you must be willing to step forward and ask this man for forgiveness as well. Take notice of how you may have neglected to show respect and love for him. Set him as a priority in your life.

Set your priorities

Making your partner a priority involves three important factors for both husbands and wives: time, desire, and consistency.

1. Time

I have encouraged you to take the time to do what is beneficial to your marriage. Time is an important factor in any healthy marriage. As we saw earlier, the beginning of your relationship probably involved talking for hours. Spending time together was so important that you would do anything in order to meet with this special person. You both took time to engage on a personal level regarding what was important to each of you. Nurturing one another was central to your relationship.

As your marriage matured, you have perhaps spent less time together. You now need to intentionally create time to be with each other. You need to look at your spouse and say honestly, "I want to spend time with you again."

Connecting with each other in your marriage is vital to reestablishing goals and objectives for the life with your spouse. It can be achieved but only when you start together. Amos 3:3 asks, "Can two people walk to-gether without agreeing on the direction?" (NLT). The relationship of marriage requires a unity that is cemented in an intimate bond to each other and to God. This means changing events and situations that would hinder the two of you from being together. Genuine dialogue requires a commitment of time.

Many other factors are important to a healthy marriage, but time together must be a priority.

Many other factors are important to a healthy marriage, but time together must be a priority. Both quantity and quality of time are needed. This will require diligence on the part of both of you. Work, kids, family activities, and church duties require time also, but none of these are more important than God's purpose in placing the two of you together. Now is the time to reconnect with your mate and refocus on each other while eliminating any outside activity that would destroy your ability to spend time together.

2. Desire

At the most basic level, desire is a longing to be with someone. Your desire to be with your spouse must become stronger than ever. You should make it clear to your spouse that you need to hear, understand, and be with him or her. Active listening is essential, i.e., listening with your whole heart. If you have lost the desire to do this with your mate, ask God to create in you a new heart and a new longing for your husband or wife.

> **Ask God to take away from you whatever has displaced your spouse.**

If your greatest desire is to be with someone or something else, ask God to take that desire away. With all sincerity, ask him to take away from you whatever has displaced your spouse. Serve your spouse with increased fervor. Fall in love with him or her all over again. Arrive home with a new desire to spend an evening with your mate, and do it with consistency in your words and behavior.

I remember the early days of my marriage. I would come home from work and stop at the end of our driveway to pick up the mail. Entering the house, with the dogs barking and the kids playing, I would proceed into the kitchen to begin sorting and opening the mail. It was as if the mail had become top priority. My wife would try to get my attention as she was preparing dinner. Being a teacher, she always had something interesting to share concerning the day with her school children, or even about our own children. I would appear to listen with that "psychologist's half ear," but the whole time I was focused on the mail. Before long, I developed a habit of not listening to my wife at all, focusing instead on the mail, which seemed to be something I needed to do. But which was more important, the mail or my wife and children? I never received the winning numbers from the Publishers Clearing House! The mail was always full of bills, junk mail, or advertisements. So why did it become so important?

Clearly, the mail was not that important, but we tend to concentrate on whatever is in front of us out of habit, habits that need to be broken and changed. Reconnecting with our spouses involves making everything else wait so you can concentrate on the person in front of you, your spouse. God has placed this special gift in your life as a priority. Neglecting this priority is wrong. Silly habits can be changed, if you are willing. Husbands, wives, are you paying attention? Do you understand what is in front of you? Are you willing to change?

3. Consistency

Marriage takes consistent time and effort. Consistency requires staying on task, even when you are tired or fatigued. Consistency means taking the actions that you know to be right, no matter how difficult they are. Look to God to lead you in this. By rebuilding your marriage together with your spouse—by refocusing on the physical, emotional, and spiritual areas of your relationship—your marriage will turn into a love affair again. It is possible if you both commit yourselves to start today to be "one flesh" and "one mind" again.

Rebuilding hope

The apostle Paul wrote that "we should not trust in ourselves but in God" (2 Cor 1:9 NKJV). He referred to our hope in the resurrection of the physical body, but I believe it also applies to the resurrection of a marriage. The future of your marriages depends on hope, and your hope depends on God.

Webster defines hope as "a desire with expectation of fulfillment." Hope is to anticipate a real answer, not a dream; it is to expect a reality, not a wish. "Now faith is being sure of what we hope for and certain of what we do not see," according Hebrews 11:1. Hope and faith based upon God's promises will renew your marriage on an ongoing basis. That is not wishful thinking. Contentment, peace, and joy can be a reality in your marriage because you serve this kind of God.

Christian hope looks ahead, not behind. Christian hope dispels the darkness from your troubled marriage and restores light. Begin today to put the pages of this book into action, based upon your confidence in God's redeeming power for you and your marriage.

I have cited the following verse throughout this book, but it bears repeating one more time: "Each one of you also must love his wife as he loves himself, and the wife must respect her husband" (Eph 5:33). God expects us husbands to be open and caring, sensitive and protective of our wives' needs. We don't need to be macho and controlling for our wives to feel safe and secure. As Paul says, we need to love, respect, and cherish our wives. Being attentive and focused on our mates, listening and reflecting on what they say, allows us to understand their needs.

If you are willing to incorporate what you have read into your own marriage, God will restore the love you once had. Your wife needs your arms around her to caress her and to shelter her from the storms that envelop her. But she can trust you only when what she sees is real. Lift her up and cherish her. Reestablish through your daily behavior the security and trust that she has been hoping for. This will allow her to be thankful for having married a man like you. When you provide genuine security, trust, and respect for your wife, you will create the opportunity for her to respect you and give honor to you, with renewed confidence that you are her best friend.

Ladies, are you listening? Are you praying for your husband, asking God to reveal what he needs from you? As you have studied this book together, have you looked for opportunities to grow again with your husband? We are talking about hope here, not discouragement, because we are talking about God's promises. Are you listening?

God can change your heart and change your husband's heart. Can you humble yourself to love this man again? Lie next to him. Pray for him and let go of the bitterness in your heart. Can you truly say, "Honey, I love you"? Can you look at him with a spirit of encouragement, letting go of the difficulties and insecurities of the past? Is the mind of Christ now beginning again to shine brightly in the darkness you thought was hopeless?

Jesus says, "Take my yoke upon you and learn from me, for I am gentle and humble in heart, and you will find rest for your souls" (Matt 11:29). The peace you seek for your marriage is found only in God. He desires to transform you and your marriage. He desires to flood your life with joy and contentment. My hope for you—in fact, my prayer for you—is that the desire for change will be so great that you will see God as never before in your life, and you will rest in his presence. God calls both of you to humble yourselves before him, praying openly for change, asking him to take away any pride and selfishness that has hindered your marriage. If you confess to God your need for him to change you, he will change you.

God calls both of you to humble yourselves before him, praying openly for change.

King David of Israel was a man after God's own heart. Yet David sinned against God in ways that most of us can never imagine. David brought a married woman into his house in order to have sex with her. Then, to cover up his sin, he brought the husband home from war and encouraged him to have sexual relations with her in order to cover up the fact that she was pregnant with David's child. When this did not work, David made sure that the betrayed husband died in battle and then married his widow so that no one would know. As we look at this atrocity, it seems unbelievable that God could hear David's confession of his sin and forgive him. But God did. This is the God we serve, a God who restored David and will restore you as well. David prayed in Psalm 51:7–8:

> Cleanse me with hyssop, and I will be clean;
>> wash me, and I will be whiter than snow.
> Let me hear joy and gladness;
>> let the bones you have crushed rejoice.

He goes on to ask in verse 10:

> Create in me a pure heart, O God,
>> And renew a steadfast spirit within me.

David's relationship with God was restored and so was his marriage. Seems impossible, doesn't it? We serve a God who deals with the impossible. Ask God to reveal what has been missing in your marriage. If there has been sin and destructiveness in your marriage, ask God to give you a clean heart, washing all bitterness away. Let him purify your spirit and your heart. God wants to open your eyes and reveal a marriage the way it was intended to be and what it can be.

Are you seeking God for the restoration of your marriage? He can accomplish something that you thought was impossible. Continually, consistently asking God to show his precious promises will allow you to love your spouse in a whole new way. It will not be an easy road, but you can travel it together with your spouse as God enables you.

Be open to change. The unknown can be frightening for all of us, but do not retreat because of fear. Know that God cares for you. Rest upon his arms. He will renew your strength and fulfill his promises for your marriage. He will rekindle your love affair with your spouse again.

A final word

As you have read through the pages of this book, my hope and prayer for you both is that you realize that joy and laughter can return to your marriage.

Men, I know how difficult it is to be a good loving husband with all the demands and expectations society places upon us. I know it is not your desire to be complacent in being a faithful husband. Don't give up. Shift the car back into drive, asking God to give you strength, wisdom, and insight for your marriage like never before. Seek help if you get stuck. Do not feel that you are alone: You are not! There *is* help.

Wives, love your husbands. Encourage him, pray for him, treat him with the respect he needs and desires. You are on this journey together. No more detours.

May God bless you both. Love *will* live again.

 Don't forget to complete the Diagnostic Evaluation on the next page.

DIAGNOSTIC EVALUATION

I challenge both of you to do three simple things each day to make an opening for God's restorative power in your marriage:

1. Pray together, asking God to create a servant's heart in you.

2. Begin the day with a kiss, a hug, a touch—a simple physical expression of affection.

3. Tell your spouse how much she or he has blessed your life.